2nd edition

openMind

Workbook

Ingrid Wisniewska

Concept development:
Mariela Gil Vierma

Level 2

MACMILLAN

Macmillan Education
4 Crinan Street
London N1 9XW
A division of Macmillan Publishers Limited

Companies and representatives throughout the world

ISBN 978-0-230-45770-6 with key
ISBN 978-0-230-45955-7 without key

This edition published 2014
First edition published 2010

Designed by emc design limited
Illustrated by Peter Cornwell page 9, 21, 24, 35, 39, 42 (Ex 5A); Sally
Elford page 5, 19, 36, 41, 69; Niall Harding (Beehive Illustration) page 42
(Ex 4C); Paul Williams (Sylvie Poggio Artists) page 27, 51, 54, 57, 73.
Cover design by emc design limited
Cover photograph by Getty Images / Blue Jean Images
Picture research by Alison Prior

Author's acknowledgements
The author would like to thank the schools, teachers and students
whose input has been invaluable in preparing this new edition. She
would also like to thank the editorial and design teams at Macmillan for
doing such a great job of organizing the material and bringing it to life.

The publishers would like to thank the following educators and
institutions who reviewed materials and provided us with invaluable
insight and feedback for the development of the Open Mind series:

Carolina Ezeta, Universidad Tecnológica de Querétaro; Karl Schmack,
Centro Cultural Costarricense Norteamericano; Maria Elisabeth Schmid
de Mattos, ICBEU – São José dos Campos; Martha Patricia Sánchez,
Colegio Anahuac Revolución; Leigh Darlaine Langenegger, ICBEU
– São José dos Campos; Ricardo Pizelli Goiatá, Curso Bridge over
Cam; Franklin Téllez, Centro Cultural Nicaragüense Norteamericano;
Jim Nixon, Colegio Cervantes Costa Rica; Rosario Mena, Instituto
Cultural Dominico Americano; Leticia de la Peña, Colegio Lincoln;
Héctor Sánchez, PROULEX; Eric Tejeda, PROULEX; Arturo Hernández,
Instituto Tecnológico de Estudios Superiores de Monterrey, Campus
Guadalajara; Grisel del Rosario, Instituto Cultural Dominico Americano;
Maria do Socorro Guimarães, IBEU – Rio de Janeiro; Diego Medina,
Universidad de Guadalajara, Licenciatura de Idiomas; Julio Prin, Centro
Venezolano Americano; María Guadalupe Muñoz, Universidad de
Guadalajara, Licenciatura de Idiomas; Lourdes Molleda, Tec Milenio;
Frances Gritzewsky, Prepa Tec Eugenio Garza; Magneli Villanueva
Morales, Universidad Regiomontana; Anderson Lopes Siqueira, ICBEU
– São José dos Campos; Emilia Rubenova, Universidad Autónoma
de Nuevo León; Lourdes Pérez Valdespino, Universidad Del Valle
de México, María Eugenia Rodríguez, Centro Cultural Salvadoreño
Americano; Márcia Soares Guimarães, Instituto Cultural Brasil Estados
Unidos -Belo Horizonte; Leonor Rosales, Instituto Tecnológico de
Estudios Superiores de Monterrey; Martha Larraga, Unitec Escobedo;
Cândido Prado, CCBEU – Goiânia; Janet Keyser, Instituto Tecnológico
de Estudios Superiores de Monterrey, Campus Cuidad de México; Julie
Khatcherian, Manhattan Trade Language Company; Francisco Nieto,
Universidad Metropolitana; Artemisa Sangermán, Instituto Tecnológico
de Estudios Superiores de Monterrey, Campus Cuidad de México;
Nico Wieserma, Instituto Tecnológico de Estudios Superiores de
Monterrey, Campus Cuidad de México; Vagner Serafim, Centro Cultural
Brasil Estados Unidos; Lourdes Baledón, Universidad Intercontinental;
Clara Lucía López, Centro Colombo Americano Manizales; Gabriela
Rodríguez, Colegio Oviedo Schontal; Waldo Andrade, CBI: Centro
Butantã Idiomas – São Paulo; Anthony Shull, Instituto Tecnológico de
Estudios Superiores de Monterrey, Campus Estado de México; Tamara
Rojas, Escuela Benjamín Franklin; Martha Rosas, Universidad del Valle
de México, Campus San Rafael; Fabiano Cella, Universidade de São
Paulo, curso Poliglota; Sheila Moreno, Universidad del Valle de México,
Campus Tlalpan; Patricia Venegas, Universidad del Valle de México,
Campus Lomas Verdes; Luciana Guarnier, Seven Idiomas; Diana Jones,
Angloamericano; Carlos Lizárraga, Angloamericano; Emma Domínguez,
The Anglo; Luis Cabrera, Universidad Nacional Autónoma de México;
Luciane Oliveira, New York School; Cristina Moya, Colegio Morelos;
Elda Beraza, Colegio Montes de Oca, Cuernavaca; Elza Massae Sato,
FMU, São Paulo; Lucía Canseco Campoy, Instituto Tecnológico de
Estudios Superiores de Monterrey, Campus Hermosillo; Emma Luisa
Domínguez Instituto Tecnológico de Estudios Superiores de Monterrey,
Campus Obregón; Yolanda Domínguez del Instituto Tecnológico de
Estudios Superiores de Monterrey, Campus Obregón; Maria Antonieta
Gagliardi, Centro Britânico – São Paulo; David Toledo, Universidad
Autónoma de Baja California; Alicia Cabrero, Universidad Autónoma
San Luis Potosí; Danielle Sales, Senac – Rio de Janeiro; Claudio Barros,
Flex Idiomas; Rina de Góngora, del Instituto Guatemalteco Americano;
Adriana Alcalá, Kate Cory-Wright, Chris Bauer; Moisés Ramírez;
Universidad Chauhtémoc Centro de Lenguas y Lingüística Aplicada,
Universidad Autonoma de Tamaulipas; Instituto Tecnológico Centro
Americano; CELE Mascarones; Ministerio de Educación de El Salvador;
Universidad Tecnológica de Nezahualcoyotl; Universidad del Tepeyac;
Instituto Politécnico Nacional ESIME CELEX; Instituto Quebec; Colegio
La Salle del Pedregal; Universidad Pedagógica Nacional; Universidad
de la República Mexicana; Universidad Norteamericana; Fundación
Empresarial para el Desarrollo Educativo; Operadora La Salle; Seven
São Paulo; Universidad de Oriente; UNIVA; Centro de Capacitación
Manuel Sandoval Vallarta; Universidad de El Salvador; Escuela de
Jurisprudencia; Universidad de Valle de México, Campus Puebla;
Alumni São Paulo; Dr. Amany Shawkey, Mrs. Heidi Omara, Mrs. Hala
Fouad (Egypt); Faisal Mreish (Lebanon); Mrs. Magda Giomazi (Libya).

Petra Florianová, Gymnázium, Praha 6, Arabská 14; Inés Frigerio,
Universidad Nacional de Río Cuarto; Alison Greenwood, University of
Bologna, Centro Linguistico di Ateneo; Roumyana Yaneva Ivanova,
The American College of Sofia; Táňa Jančaříková, SOŠ Drtinova
Prague; Mari Carmen Lafuente, Escuela Oficial de Idiomas Hospitalet,
Barcelona; Alice Lockyer, Pompeu Fabra University; Javier Roque
Sandro Majul, Windmill School of English; Paul Neale, Susan Carol
Owens and Beverley Anne Sharp, Cambridge Academy of English;
Audrey Renton, Dubai Men's College, Higher Colleges of Technology,
UAE; Martin Stanley, British Council, Bilbao; Luiza Wójtowicz-Waga,
Warsaw Study Centre; Escuela Oficial de Idiomas de Getxo; Cámara
de Comercio de Bilbao; Universidad Autónoma de Bellaterra; Escuela
Oficial de Idiomas EOI de Barcelona; University of Barcelona; Escuela
Oficial de Idiomas Sant Gervasi.

Printed and bound in Thailand

2018 2017 2016 2015 2014
11 10 9 8 7 6 5 4 3 2

CONTENTS

UNIT 1   NEW MILLENNIUM

1 VOCABULARY: internet activities

A 👂 **01** **Listen and complete the conversation with the internet activities.**

Sarah: What do you mainly use your laptop for?

Doug: Oh, I (1) _____ the internet looking for new music and music websites.

Sarah: Do you shop (2) _____?

Doug: Yes, I often (3) _____ songs that I like and put them on my MP3 player.

Sarah: What about social media? How often do you use sites like Facebook, for example?

Doug: A lot. I'm in a band and we have a Facebook page. I use it to (4) _____ pictures or (5) _____ videos of our concerts. We also use it to (6) _____ about what we're doing as a band.

Sarah: How about Twitter—do you (7) _____ a lot?

Doug: All the time! It's a great way to get publicity.

Sarah: Great! So it's easy to find you then?

Doug: Sure! Just (8) _____ our name—the Martian Rockets!

B **Complete the questions with phrases in the box.**

blog browse download post shop upload

1 Do you like to _____ online for clothes?
2 Do you keep a diary or _____ about your life online?
3 Do you ever _____ videos onto YouTube?
4 Do you prefer to _____ music from the internet or buy CDs?
5 How often do you _____ pictures online?
6 What search engine do you like to use to _____ the internet?

C **Choose one of the questions from Exercise B and write your answer. Explain why.**

I prefer to buy clothes online because it is fast and easy.

_____

2 GRAMMAR: past progressive

A Write the *-ing* form of the verbs.

1 go   *going*
2 play   _____
3 swim   _____
4 write   _____
5 dance   _____

B Read the information in the table. Complete the sentences and questions.

What were you doing yesterday afternoon?	Bruno	Vanessa	_____
chat with friends online	✓	✗	
shop online	✓	✓	
download music	✓	✗	
send emails	✗	✗	
study English	✓	✓	

1 Bruno _____ with friends online yesterday.
2 He _____ emails.
3 Vanessa _____ with friends online yesterday.
4 She _____ online.
5 A: _____ Bruno _____ online?
   B: _____, he _____.
6 A: _____ Vanessa _____ music?
   B: _____, she _____.
7 A: _____ Bruno and Vanessa _____ emails?
   B: _____, they _____.
8 A: _____ Bruno and Vanessa _____ English?
   B: _____, they _____.

C Now complete the survey in Exercise B for you. Then write three sentences about what you were or weren't doing online yesterday.

D Complete the comments with the past progressive form of the verbs in the box.

celebrate	listen	play	send	not sleep	watch

What were you doing at midnight on New Year's Eve?

Ben: I _____ with friends.
Sam: We _____ to an amazing band.
Louise: I _____ because there was so much noise.
Gina: I _____ TV, and my brother _____ a computer game.
Vicky: I _____ emails to all my friends!

> ### WATCH OUT!
>
> ✗ He wasn't do his homework this morning.
>
> ✓ _____

3 VOCABULARY: describing reactions

A Circle the best adjective to complete each sentence.

1 You dropped my laptop! I'm really angry / surprised with you.
2 My new computer can download files really fast! I'm upset / amazed by it.
3 You loved your car, but you sold it! I'm surprised / worried by it.
4 I bought a new cell phone yesterday. I'm so excited / angry about it.
5 Nancy's favorite team won the game. She's upset / happy about it.
6 Our dog broke its leg. My son is very excited / upset about it.
7 I found a new website for shopping online. I'm very interested / angry in it.
8 I think I failed my test. I'm very surprised / worried about it.

B 🎧 02 Listen to people talking about events in the past. How did they feel about them? Write an adjective to describe their reactions.

4 READING: pronoun reference

A Complete the sentences with the correct pronouns for the words in bold.

1 **My sister and I** went to our first **concert** when we were 12. _____ had a great time. _____ was so exciting.
2 **Hannah and her family** took a **vacation** in Mexico and they really enjoyed _____. _____ went there in April.
3 **Penny and Dan** invited **Sarah** to their housewarming party. _____ gave _____ some flowers as a housewarming gift.
4 **Anna** sent an **email** to David. _____ wrote _____ during her lunch break.

B Read Julia's blog about an event she went to recently. What do the pronouns in bold refer to? Choose the correct option below.

On New Year's Eve, I went to a concert with my friends. **(1) It** finished very late and **(2) we** were waiting outside with a lot of other fans when some of the band members walked by. **(3) They** said hello to us and asked our names! I was so excited! I took a picture with my cell phone and they signed my concert ticket! I'm going to hang **(4) it** on my bedroom wall.

1 **a)** the band **b)** the concert
2 **a)** Julia and her friends **b)** Julia
3 **a)** the band **b)** the fans
4 **a)** the picture **b)** the ticket

5 GRAMMAR: past progressive and simple past

A Complete the sentences with the simple past or past progressive form of the verbs in parentheses.

1 Sumiko _____ (live) in Canada when she _____ (write) her first book.

2 We _____ (get) the idea for our restaurant while we _____ (travel) in Mexico.

3 While Adriana _____ (study) in the library, someone _____ (steal) her cell phone.

4 Sarah and Mike _____ (clean) the house when they _____ (find) a large box of old letters from their grandmother.

5 When Joanna _____ (meet) her husband, she _____ (study) to be a doctor.

6 While I _____ (research) online, I _____ (find) a good website for meeting old school friends.

B There is one mistake in each sentence. Find and correct it.

1 I was chat online when I heard the crash.

_____

2 We didn't go out while it were raining.

_____

3 Julianne and Kate were have dinner when they heard the news.

_____

4 Did you living in South Korea when you started Korean lessons?

_____

> ### WATCH OUT!
> ✗ What you were doing when I called you?
>
> ✓ _____

6 SPEAKING: asking follow-up questions

Complete the conversations with questions in the box.

> And what about you?   Cool. Did you like it?
> Oh, yeah? How come?   Really? Why? What were you doing?
> Yeah? Where?

1 **A:** What were you doing in Japan?
   B: I was studying judo.
   A: _____
   B: Yes, I did. It was great.

2 **A:** Where were you living last year?
   B: I was living in Brazil.
   A: _____
   B: In Recife.

3 **A:** This time last year I was living in New York City.
   B: _____
   A: I was playing in a jazz band.

4 **A:** We took a great vacation in California last summer.
   _____
   B: Oh, I didn't have time for a vacation last year.
   A: _____
   B: I had to work on an important project.

Listen and write

A 🎧 **03** Listen to Darren talking about a key event in his life.
Answer the questions.

1 What key event is Darren describing? _____
2 How did he feel before the event? Why? _____
3 How did he feel during the event? Why? _____
4 How did he feel after the event? _____
5 What happened at the end? _____

B Think about a key event in your life. Write notes about it.

Key event: _____
1 Where was it? _____
2 What was I doing? _____
3 How was I feeling?
    (before) _____
    (during) _____
    (after) _____
4 Why was it important?

Over to You

C 🖊 Use the information from Exercise B
to write a paragraph in your notebook about
an important event in your life.

WRITING TUTOR

Choose one way to begin your paragraph:
I remember when …
A day I can never forget is the day when …
A key event in my life was when …
Choose one way to end your paragraph:
This event was important to me because …
When I remember this day/event/experience today,
I feel …
Remember to use pronoun references:
*I am still in touch with my friends. Some of **them**
write blogs online.*

DOWN TIME

A Read the clues and complete the crossword with words to describe feelings.

Across

4 Susan's boyfriend didn't call last night.
   She wasn't h … y.
5 I'm studying political science in college.
   I'm i … d in political systems.
7 Jane got a diamond necklace for her birthday.
   She was s … d.
8 Martha got a 100 on her English exam.
   She was a … d.

Down

1 Someone crashed into Dan's bicycle.
   He was a … y.
2 Eric couldn't find his wallet and his keys.
   He was w … d.
3 Ricky's girlfriend doesn't want to see him again.
   He is u … t.
6 Reiko saw her friend on TV.
   She was e … d.

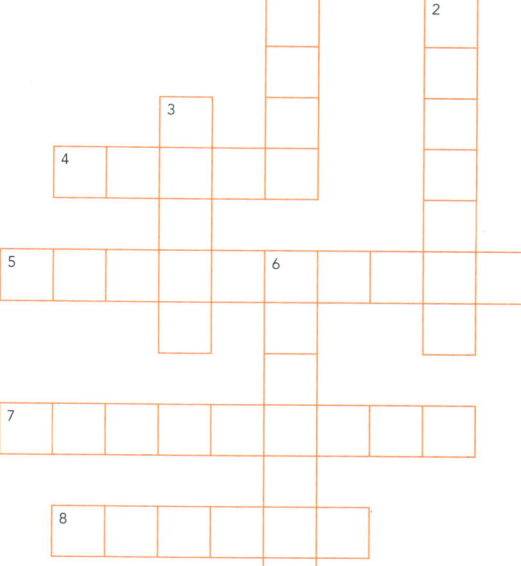

B Use the pictures to find words that rhyme with words in the box. Complete the sentences.

fine	game	hide	mice	nice	nine	ride	same

1 It's not different—it's the *same*. You can play it—it's a _____.
2 It's a bike and you can _____ it. You can't find this if I _____ it.
3 You're very happy—you feel _____. It's the number after eight—it's _____.
4 They're small animals—they're _____. They're not horrible—they're _____.

C Read the sentences aloud. Can you hear the rhymes?

UNIT 2 CULTURE VULTURE

1 VOCABULARY: adjectives for expressing opinions

A Write the adjectives in the box in the correct column of the table.

> amazing awesome dull dumb fascinating hilarious incredible
> interesting ridiculous terrible weird

Positive	Negative

B Choose the correct adjective to complete the sentences.

1 I really liked the latest *Iron Man™* movie. The action scenes were …
   a) incredible.   **b)** ridiculous.
2 I don't think this kind of art is very good. What does it mean? It's …
   a) incredible.   **b)** terrible.
3 This kind of video art is new and interesting. It's really …
   a) dull.   **b)** fascinating.
4 Many people thought the play was very funny. It was …
   a) hilarious.   **b)** weird.
5 I never go to horror movies. They're not interesting; in fact, they're …
   a) ridiculous.   **b)** fascinating.
6 This artist makes sculptures out of recycled car tires. They're definitely …
   a) hilarious.   **b)** weird.

2 GRAMMAR: comparatives with *as … as / not as … as*

A Write the words in the correct order to make sentences.

1 art galleries / aren't / Museums / as / as / interesting / .
   _____

2 isn't / easy / as / Painting / photography / as / .
   _____

3 TV shows / as / aren't / movies / good / as / .
   _____

4 dull / hip-hop / Country music / as / isn't / as / .
   _____

B Complete the sentences with the adjective in parentheses and (*not*) *as ... as.*

1 horror movies ✓ / action movies ✓ ✓ (*interesting*)
Horror movies are not as interesting as action movies.
2 opera ✓ / rock music ✓ ✓ (*exciting*)
Opera is _____.
3 classical music concerts ✓ / operas ✓ (*expensive*)
Classical music concerts are _____.
4 modern art ✓ / classical art ✓ ✓ (*well-liked*)
Modern art is _____.
5 photography ✓ / painting ✓ (*difficult*)
Photography is _____.
6 online games ✓ / video games ✓ ✓ (*popular*)
Online games are _____.

WATCH OUT!

Ⓧ CDs are expensive as DVDs.

✓ _____
_____

3 LISTENING: identifying speakers' opinions

A 🎧 **04** Listen and check the adjectives you hear in the conversation.

☐ amazing   ☐ weird   ☐ fascinating   ☐ terrible
☐ boring   ☐ dull   ☐ ridiculous   ☐ incredible

B 🎧 **05** Listen to two friends talking about a movie. Circle *T* (true) or *F* (false).

1	The man liked the movie.	T / F
2	The man loves comedies.	T / F
3	The man thinks comedies aren't as good as action movies.	T / F
4	The woman liked the movie.	T / F
5	The woman says the movie was as good as the director's last movie.	T / F

4 VOCABULARY: cultural activities

A Choose the best words to complete the sentences.

1 I'd like to join an exhibition / a music society.
2 I'd like to take a language class / a museum.
3 I'd like to go to a book club / a comedy show.
4 I'd like to learn about architecture / a language class.
5 I'd like to go to see an exhibition / a photography course.

B Complete the conversations with words in the box.

1 **Becky:** Hi, Judy! Would you like to _____ to the theater with me tomorrow evening?
   Judy: Sure!

2 **Jane:** We both really love music. Let's _____ a music society!
   Mary: Good idea!

3 **Mike:** I want to _____ more about art.
   Georgia: Why don't we go to _____ an exhibition this weekend at the Academy of Arts and then _____ an art course there or something?

go
join
learn
see
take

5 GRAMMAR: superlatives

A Complete the table with the superlative form of the adjectives.

Adjective	Superlative	Adjective	Superlative
good		strange	
bad		popular	
funny		happy	
fat		interesting	
beautiful		important	

B Read the information in the bar graph. Then complete the sentences on the next page with the superlative form of the adjective in parentheses.

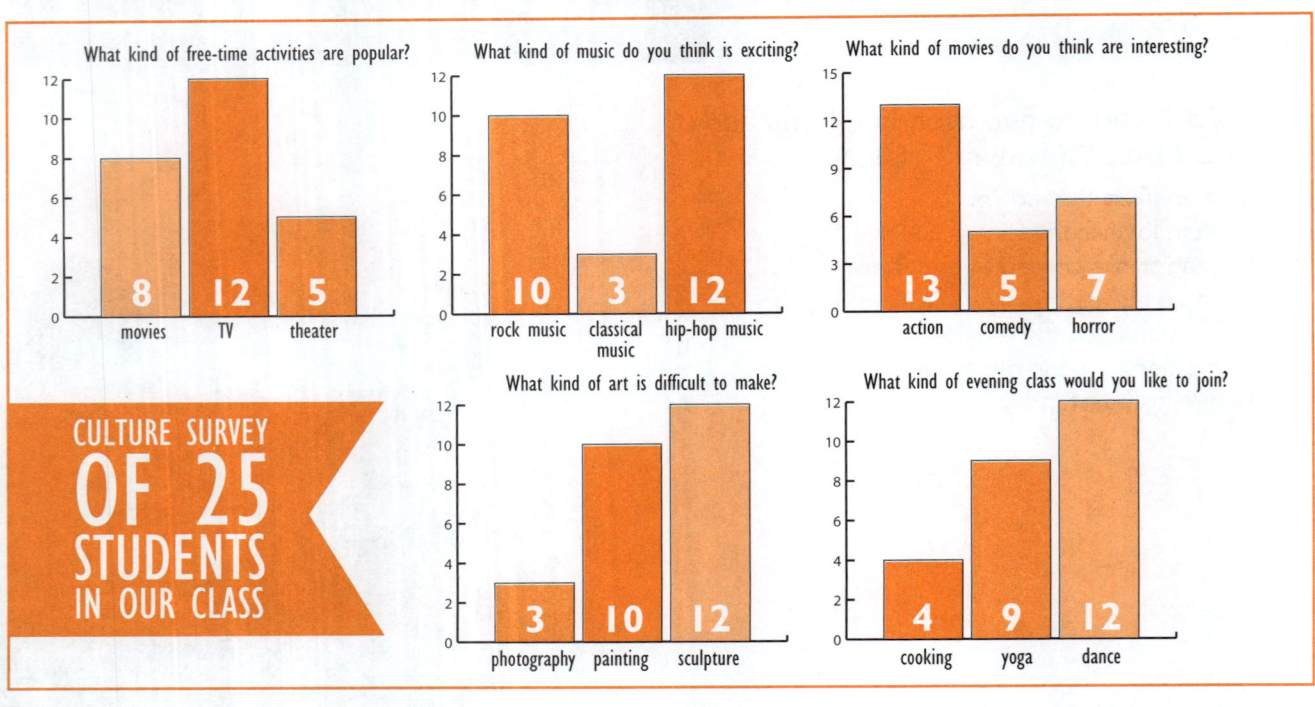

CULTURE SURVEY OF 25 STUDENTS IN OUR CLASS

What kind of free-time activities are popular? — movies 8, TV 12, theater 5

What kind of music do you think is exciting? — rock music 10, classical music 3, hip-hop music 12

What kind of movies do you think are interesting? — action 13, comedy 5, horror 7

What kind of art is difficult to make? — photography 3, painting 10, sculpture 12

What kind of evening class would you like to join? — cooking 4, yoga 9, dance 12

1 Going to the theater is the *least popular* (*popular*) free-time activity for these students.
2 Hip-hop music is the _____ (*exciting*) kind of music in the class.
3 They think that action movies are the _____ (*boring*) kind of movies.
4 They think that classical music is the _____ (*exciting*) kind of music.
5 They think that comedies are the _____ (*interesting*) kind of movies.
6 They think that sculpture is the _____ (*difficult*) kind of art to make.
7 Watching TV is the _____ (*popular*) free-time activity in the class.
8 They think that dance is the _____ (*good*) kind of class.

WATCH OUT!

(X) Photography is the most easiest kind of art to make.

(✓) _____
_____

C Complete the sentences about art and entertainment in your country. Use the superlative form for each of the adjectives in the box. You can use each adjective more than once.

| exciting | famous | funny | good | popular |

1 *Mad Men* is *the most popular* TV series.
2 _____ is _____ TV show.
3 _____ is _____ singer.
4 _____ is _____ actor.
5 _____ is _____ writer.
6 _____ is _____ sport.

6 WRITING: linking sentences

A Match the beginnings 1–4 with the endings a–d.

1 Phone calls can be expensive so
2 Music is important to me because
3 I love modern art so
4 Foreign movies are interesting because

a) it helps me feel relaxed and happier.
b) I can learn about other cultures.
c) I prefer to send text messages.
d) I go to a gallery once a month.

B Complete the conversation with *because* or *so*.

Pamela: Why weren't you in art class last night?
Mike: **(1)** _____ I went to the theater with my family. It was my sister's birthday. She loves musicals, **(2)** _____ we went to see *The Phantom of the Opera*.
Pamela: Really! Was it good?
Mike: Yes, I enjoyed it, but I don't like missing our art classes. **(3)** _____, you know, art is my favorite subject.
Pamela: I know, but yesterday the teacher was sick **(4)** _____ we all went to the art gallery. It was great!

Read and write

A Read Max's movie review. Then answer the questions.

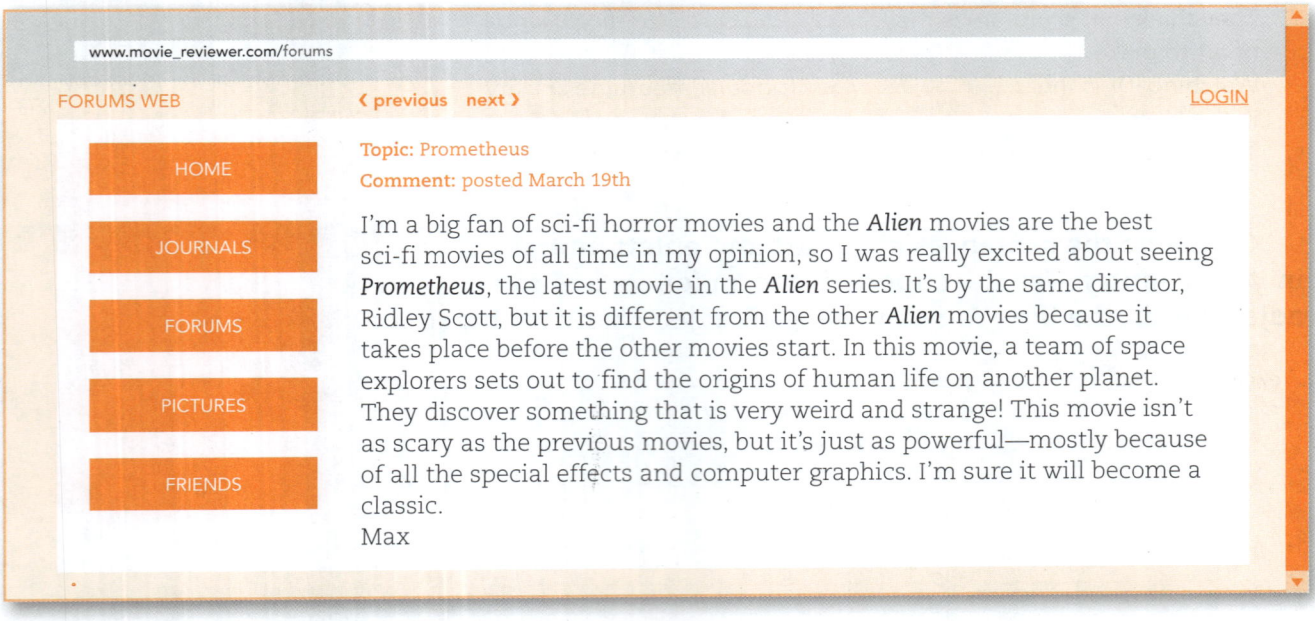

www.movie_reviewer.com/forums

FORUMS WEB   ‹ previous   next ›   LOGIN

HOME

JOURNALS

FORUMS

PICTURES

FRIENDS

Topic: Prometheus
Comment: posted March 19th

I'm a big fan of sci-fi horror movies and the *Alien* movies are the best sci-fi movies of all time in my opinion, so I was really excited about seeing *Prometheus*, the latest movie in the *Alien* series. It's by the same director, Ridley Scott, but it is different from the other *Alien* movies because it takes place before the other movies start. In this movie, a team of space explorers sets out to find the origins of human life on another planet. They discover something that is very weird and strange! This movie isn't as scary as the previous movies, but it's just as powerful—mostly because of all the special effects and computer graphics. I'm sure it will become a classic.
Max

1 What is the name of the movie? _____
2 What kind of movie is it? _____
3 What is different about this movie? _____
4 Does the reviewer like it? Why or why not? _____

B Choose a movie that you saw recently and answer the questions.

1 What kind of movie is it? _____
2 What is it about? _____
3 What is special about it? _____
4 Write three adjectives to describe the movie and say why you chose them.
   The movie is _____ because _____.
   It is _____ because _____.
   It is _____ because _____.

Over to You

C ✎ Write a paragraph in your notebook describing your opinion of the movie you chose in Exercise B.

WRITING TUTOR

I think this movie is exciting because …
This movie is not as … as other (action)
movies because …
This movie is very … so I think that …

DOWN TIME

A **Take the culture quiz. Choose the correct answer.**

1   Van Gogh was a famous …
    a) artist.   **b)** sculptor.
2   Charles Dickens was a famous …
    a) photographer.   **b)** writer.
3   Johnny Depp is a famous …
    a) writer.   **b)** actor.
4   Coco Chanel was a famous …
    a) fashion designer.   **b)** artist.
5   Mozart was a famous …
    a) composer.   **b)** dancer.
6   Green Day is a famous …
    a) theater group.   **b)** rock band.

7   Pavarotti was a famous …
    a) singer.   **b)** musician.
8   The *Mona Lisa* is a famous …
    a) painting.   **b)** sculpture.
9   *The Sound of Music* is a famous …
    a) musical.   **b)** novel.
10 The Louvre is a famous …
    a) theater.   **b)** art museum.

B **Find the words and write them under the correct picture. The words can go forward (→), down (↓), or diagonally (↗).**

Y	T	F	G	R	E	B	I	H	T	C	O	P	H	V
J	N	I	E	P	A	D	U	T	N	L	S	E	O	K
A	B	A	L	L	E	T	X	H	L	A	T	R	R	D
O	R	L	I	U	E	J	A	E	O	S	Z	U	R	J
Z	A	T	T	E	R	U	P	W	U	S	K	I	O	E
R	S	S	E	F	Z	I	S	X	F	I	T	T	R	F
D	D	Y	R	X	H	B	A	C	D	C	A	E	M	K
E	L	O	A	I	H	N	I	M	S	A	O	A	O	O
G	W	P	T	H	R	I	J	N	Z	L	N	S	V	Y
F	T	H	U	V	O	X	B	V	T	M	C	S	I	W
A	T	G	R	O	R	E	A	I	L	U	R	E	E	D
B	I	P	E	M	C	L	L	Q	T	S	F	T	S	P
I	J	E	T	X	C	M	E	U	F	I	H	K	Y	H
X	N	A	R	S	D	Y	T	N	P	C	O	L	F	N
R	D	M	U	J	B	N	T	V	C	I	U	N	W	H

1   _ _ _ _ _ _ _

2   _ _ _ _ _ _ _ _ _
    _ _ _ _ _ _ _ _ _

3   _ _ _ _ _

4   _ _ _ _ _ _ _
    _ _ _ _ _ _ _

5   _ _ _ _ _ _
    _ _ _ _ _ _ _

UNIT 3 TICKETS, MONEY, PASSPORT!

A))) 06 **What are these people taking with them on vacation? Listen and write the correct words below each picture. Check the spelling in your Student's Book or a dictionary.**

_____
_____
_____

B **Complete the sentences with words from Exercise A.**

1 You need a _____ to brush your teeth.
2 You need a _____ to enter another country.
3 You need a _____ to rent and drive a car.
4 You need a _____ to get on the plane.
5 You need a _____ to find the best places to visit.
6 You need a _____ to keep your money in.
7 You need a _____ to carry your clothes.
8 You need a _____ to plan your trip and find your way.

C **Choose two essential items for each trip from the items in Exercise B.**

1 a skiing trip in the Rockies
  You need _____ and _____.
2 a visit to a Broadway show in New York City
  You need _____ and _____.
3 a tour of famous cities in China
  You need _____ and _____.

2 GRAMMAR: reflexive pronouns

A **Complete the sentences with the correct words in the box.**

herself	himself	myself	ourselves	themselves	yourself

1 She bought _____ a new bag.
2 They often travel by _____.
3 Do you usually repair the car _____?
4 We drove _____ to the airport.
5 I don't like living by _____.
6 He fell, but he didn't hurt _____.

B Check the correct column.

		Subject and object are the same	Without help from another person	Alone
1	I went to Hawaii by myself.			
2	We booked the hotel ourselves.			
3	He talks to himself a lot.			
4	They planned the trip themselves.			
5	Did you hurt yourself when you lifted those bags?			
6	She doesn't like traveling by herself.			

C Complete the conversation with reflexive pronouns.

Jane: Where are you and Samantha going for your next vacation?

Phil: We're going on a road trip to Mexico!

Jane: Awesome! Are you going with friends or by **(1)** _____?

Phil: We're going by **(2)** _____. Samantha bought **(3)** _____ a phrase book and is studying Spanish!

Jane: Great! I went to Mexico once, but I was by **(4)** _____ and I didn't enjoy it very much.

Phil: Really? I thought you enjoyed traveling by **(5)** _____.

D There is one mistake in each sentence. Find and correct it.

1 He doesn't like traveling himself. _____

2 I'd like to pay for me, please. _____

3 We can choose the places to visit ourself. _____

4 They didn't tell us much about theirself. _____

5 Please get you something to eat. _____

6 Can he carry these bags by him? _____

3 VOCABULARY: travel

A Complete the sentences with words in the box.

change   check in   find   make   pack   rent

1 We need to _____ some money. Where's the bank?

2 Where can I _____ a good restaurant?

3 You should _____ a flight reservation before you go.

4 Don't forget to _____ your sunscreen and sunglasses.

5 Can we _____ a car at the airport?

6 What time can we _____ at the airport?

B Complete the sentences with the correct form of verbs in the box.

buy   change   check in   ~~go~~   make   pack   rent   take

TRAVEL
Six ways to plan a stress-free vacation!

1 Before I (1) *go* on vacation, I usually buy a guidebook and make a list of things to do.

2 I go online to (2) _____ a cheap plane ticket and (3) _____ a hotel reservation. It's sometimes cheaper to (4) _____ a car online, too.

3 After that, I go to the bank to (5) _____ some money. It's good to have some cash in the local currency, but I often use my credit card when I travel.

4 Then I make a list of things to (6) _____ in my backpack. This usually includes a guidebook and a map, and of course, my passport.

5 I usually (7) _____ a bus or a train to the airport because airport parking is very expensive.

6 When I get to the airport, I (8) _____ at the ticket desk as soon as possible. After that, I can relax with a cup of coffee until my plane takes off.

---

4 READING: pronoun reference

Read the ads. What does each pronoun in bold refer to? Write your answers below.

A Different Place   SEARCH

Looking for an unusual vacation? Search our site for fun ideas for your next trip!

Tree house weekend

Experience an incredible weekend in one of our beautiful tree houses. They are made of natural wood and bamboo so **they** blend into the local environment. You can see birds and animals come close to you, and you can take pictures of **them**. You can also hire one of our guides. **He**'ll make sure you have an unforgettable vacation.

Ice hotel

Enter an amazing world of snow and ice. Everything in this hotel is made of ice – including the walls and the furniture! The restaurant has ice chairs. **They**'re not for decoration – you can sit on **them** and eat dinner at ice tables! This magical hotel is open only from December to April. Then **it** disappears … until next year.

1 Tree house weekend
they: _____
them: _____
He: _____

2 Ice hotel
They: _____
them: _____
it: _____

5 GRAMMAR: modals of permission, request, and offer

A Read the questions and decide if the person is asking for permission (P), making a request (R), or making an offer (O). Circle the correct option.

1 May I see the menu, please?   P / R / O
2 Can I help you open the door?   P / R / O
3 Could I borrow your cell phone, please?   P / R / O
4 I'll call a taxi for you.   P / R / O
5 Can you show me the way to the station, please?   P / R / O

> **WATCH OUT!**
>
> ✗ May you tell me the time, please?
>
> ✓ _____

B Write the words in the correct order to make requests. Then match to where you think each one takes place.

1 have / tickets, / please / could / I / two / ?
    a) in a supermarket

2 may / cell phone / I / my / here / use / ?
    b) in the subway station

3 I / get / please, / olives / of / could / 200 g / ?
    c) in a bookstore

4 carry / you / can / suitcase / for me / my / ?
    d) at a hospital

5 pay / by credit card / could / I / ?
    e) at a hotel

6 SPEAKING: responding appropriately

A Read the responses and write P (positive) or N (negative) in the boxes.

☐ Sorry.   ☐ I'm sorry, I can't.   ☐ I'd rather you didn't.
☐ Sure.   ☐ Go ahead.   ☐ Of course.
☐ No problem.   ☐ Certainly.

B 🎧 07 Complete the conversations with expressions from Exercise A. Then listen and check.

1 **A:** Can I borrow your newspaper?
    B: _____ I'm still reading it.

2 **A:** May I sit here?
    B: Sure. _____

3 **A:** Could you open the window, please?
    B: _____ The window is broken.

4 **A:** Can you help me with my bag, please?
    B: _____ No problem.

Listen and write

A 🎧 **08** Listen to Sofia and Alex talking about their vacations. Circle **T** (true) or **F** (false).

1	Sofia and Alex went to Barbados on their vacation last year.	T / F
2	They went sightseeing and visited a lot of museums.	T / F
3	They went to the beach.	T / F
4	Sofia likes beach vacations.	T / F
5	Alex doesn't like sightseeing.	T / F
6	They agree to go somewhere different next year.	T / F

B Listen again and write a reason why each person likes going on vacation.

1 Alex: _____

2 Sofia: _____

C Think about your ideal vacation. Write notes about it.

Location	
Who with?	
Travel essentials	
Activities	

Over to You

D ✏️ Use your notes from Exercise C to write a description in your notebook of your ideal vacation.

WRITING TUTOR

For my ideal vacation, I'd like to go …
I'll take … with me because …
I love … because …

DOWN TIME

A Follow the lines to find out who owns which items. Write the words.

B Find six differences between the pictures. Write sentences to describe them.

_____

_____

_____

_____

_____

_____

UNIT 4 IT COULD HAPPEN TO ANYONE!

1 VOCABULARY: good and bad experiences

A Complete the sentences with the correct form of the verbs in the box.

| fail | find | get | have | lose | miss | see | win |

1 My team _____ the race last Saturday. We were all so excited.
2 Rob _____ an accident. He crashed his car last week.
3 I _____ my fitness-club card. I had to pay for a new one.
4 We were ten minutes late. We _____ the train.
5 I _____ a great promotion at work. I'm so happy.
6 I made a lot of mistakes. I _____ my test.
7 We waited outside the movie studios, and we _____ Angelina Jolie.
8 I looked everywhere for my keys, and then I _____ them in the washing machine!

WATCH OUT!

(X) I lost the last bus home.

(✓) _____

B Complete the questions with the correct verb. Then match sentences 1–6 to the correct answers a–f.

1 Did you *fail* your test?
2 Did you _____ your cell phone?
3 How much did he _____ in the lottery?
4 Did Jenny _____ the plane?
5 Did you _____ an accident?
6 Where did you _____ your wallet?

a) I don't know. In the park, I think.
b) Yes, I fell down the stairs.
c) Yes, she overslept.
d) About $3,000!
e) No, I got a 98! I passed.
f) Yes, it was under my bed.

2 GRAMMAR: present perfect — *ever/never*

A Complete the table.

Verb	Past participle	Verb	Past participle
be		give	
go		win	
work		read	
find		watch	
eat		see	

22

B Write the words in the correct order to make sentences.

1 eaten / never / I / have / sushi / .

_____

2 we / visited / never / Thailand / have / .

_____

3 the lottery / never / I / have / won / .

_____

4 never / she / seen / has / _Star Trek™_ / .

_____

5 an / office / worked / never / have / I / in / .

_____

6 he / newspaper / a / read / never / has / .

_____

C Write the questions using the prompts and then write your own answers.

1 you / miss / a plane
   A: _Have you ever missed a plane?_
   B: _No, I haven't._

2 you / lose / your passport
   A: _____
   B: _____

3 you / win / a competition
   A: _____
   B: _____

4 you / write / a letter
   A: _____
   B: _____

5 you / have / an accident
   A: _____
   B: _____

6 you / catch / a fish
   A: _____
   B: _____

WATCH OUT!

✗ I have never saw a giraffe.

✓ _____

3 LISTENING: identifying speakers' opinions

A 🔊 **09** Listen to the conversations. Do the people agree or disagree with each other?

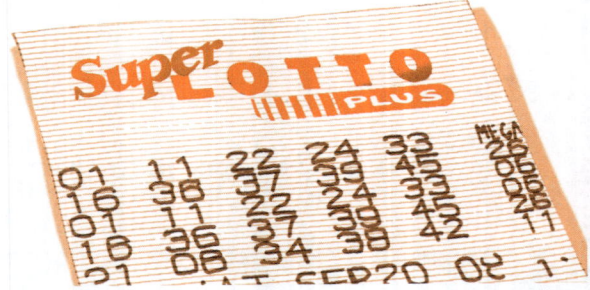

Conversation 1: agree / disagree

Conversation 2: agree / disagree

Conversation 3: agree / disagree

Conversation 4: agree / disagree

B Listen again. Write the number of the conversation by each phrase.

- ☐ I don't think so.
- ☐ I don't know.
- ☐ In my opinion, …
- ☐ That's true.
- ☐ I know.
- ☐ I think …
- ☐ Personally, I …

4 VOCABULARY: feelings

A Match the situations 1–8 to the feelings a–h.

1	Daniela got a 98 on her final exam for history.	a)	thrilled
2	I didn't understand anything because he talked too fast.	b)	uncomfortable
3	I got lost and it was getting dark.	c)	exhausted
4	Junko ran five miles without stopping.	d)	proud
5	I couldn't remember my cell phone number.	e)	disappointed
6	I have to give a speech in front of a lot of people tomorrow.	f)	confused
7	Stan spent all his money on a new CD, but it wasn't very good.	g)	embarrassed
8	We went to Los Angeles and saw our favorite band in concert.	h)	scared

B 🔊 **10** Listen to the conversations. Use key words to answer the questions.

	Conversation 1	Conversation 2	Conversation 3

What happened?			
How did the speaker feel?			

5 GRAMMAR: present perfect — *How long* and *for/since*

A Complete the table with expressions that go with *for* or *since*. Use words in the box.

2008	an hour	last year	November	six months	three days	two years	Wednesday

for							
since							

B Rewrite the sentences using the present perfect form of the verbs in parentheses.

1 The last time I went to a concert was three months ago (*go*).
   I haven't been to a concert for three months.

2 The last time Louisa went to Brazil was ten years ago. (*go*)
   She hasn't _____.

3 I started to study Chinese four years ago. (*study*)
   I've _____.

4 They moved into their new home in 2013. (*live*)
   They've _____.

5 I bought this MP3 player in August. (*have*)
   I've _____.

6 We got our cat two years ago. (*have*)
   We've _____.

> **WATCH OUT!**
>
> ✗ I've live in this town for three years.
>
> ✓ _____

C Complete the sentences with the present perfect and *for* or *since*.

1 **A:** How long _____ Tina and Damian _____ (*own*) their car?
   B: _____ three years.

2 Maria feels sleepy because she _____ (*not have*) any coffee _____ 9 o'clock.

3 I'm very hungry. I _____ (*not eat*) anything _____ last night!

4 My brother is coming to visit us tomorrow. We _____ (*not see*) him _____ five years.

5 **A:** How long _____ Ray _____ (*play*) basketball?
   B: _____ he was four.

6 Teresa teaches yoga at the community center. She _____ (*teach*) there _____ two years.

6 WRITING: linking sentences

A Complete the sentences with *and, but, or, so,* and *because*.

1 I've never eaten Thai food, _____ my sister has eaten it many times.
2 Peter has lived in the Caribbean for three years _____ he has bought a new house there.
3 I'm really embarrassed. I failed my driving test _____ I couldn't park.
4 I think he is either a musician _____ an actor. I'm not sure.
5 Sacha loves Italian art _____ I bought her a book about it for her birthday.

B Complete the sentences with your own ideas.

1 I like to _____ and _____.
2 I would like to _____ because _____.
3 I often _____, but _____.
4 I want to _____ or _____.
5 I love _____ so _____.

It could happen to anyone!   **UNIT 4   25**

Read and write

A Match the topics to the paragraphs. Then complete the survey.

1 ☐ I missed a plane.
2 ☐ I went bungee jumping.

MEMORABLE EXPERIENCES

We asked our readers about their unusual experiences. Here's what they said:

a "It was in Canada in 2009. It was one of the most exciting things I've ever done. We climbed up a mountain and walked onto a very high bridge. It was 500 feet high, and there was a river below. When I looked down, I was really scared. But I closed my eyes and jumped. It felt like flying. It was really amazing. I'm proud I did it, and I have more confidence, but I wouldn't want to do it again."

b "It was horrible. I was coming home from vacation, and someone stole my passport and wallet on the bus to the airport. I couldn't get home. I waited in the airport for my parents to send me some money, but it took two days for the money to arrive. I've never felt so exhausted in my life. It was the worst experience I've ever had, but I'm more careful now."

Tell us about your experiences and we'll publish the best ones in our next issue.

What happened? _____

Where did it happen? _____

When did it happen? _____

How did you feel? _____

Have you done it since then? _____

Over to You

B ✎ Use your notes from the survey to write a paragraph in your notebook about your unusual experience.

WRITING TUTOR

Choose one of these ways to start:
I once had a weird experience when I was …
The most unusual experience I have ever had was when …

Choose one of these ways to finish:
I'll never forget that experience because …
That's an experience that I will always remember because …

Check your work:
Did you use linking words and, but, or, because, and so in your writing?

DOWN TIME

A Read the clues and complete the crossword.

Across

2. Oh, no! I've … my keys. Where are they?
4. I've never … octopus before. It's delicious!
8. Have you … your new bicycle yet?
9. I haven't … you for ages! How are you?
10. I'm not lucky. I've never … the lottery.

Down

1. I've never … in a hot air balloon.
3. How long have you … the guitar?
5. I haven't … any coffee today.
6. Have you ever … to Thailand?
7. Have you ever … a train?

B Write the words to describe feelings. Unscramble the shaded letters to find the mystery word.

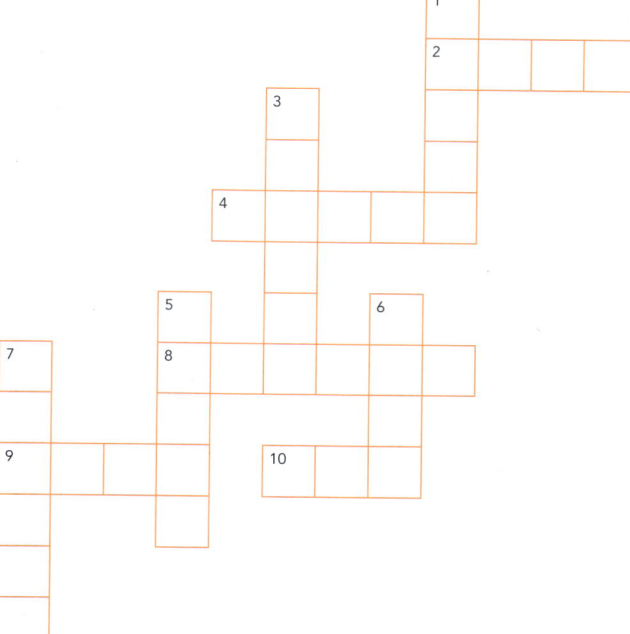

1. She won first prize. She is ___ ___ ___ ___ ___ ___.
2. He doesn't understand. He's ___ ___ ___ ___ ___ ___ ___ ___ ___.
3. The concert is canceled. She's ___ ___ ___ ___ ___ ___ ___ ___ ___ ___ ___.
4. He forgot your name. He's ___ ___ ___ ___ ___ ___ ___ ___ ___.
5. She passed her driver's test. She's ___ ___ ___ ___ ___ ___ ___ ___ ___.
6. He's afraid. He's ___ ___ ___ ___ ___ ___ ___.
7. He's very tired. He's ___ ___ ___ ___ ___ ___ ___ ___.

Mystery word: ___ ___ ___ ___ ___ ___ ___ ___

UNIT 5 MUSICAL NOTES

A Unscramble the words to find the names of different types of music.

1 l a l a c s i s c   _____
2 e a g r e g   _____
3 y e v a h l e m t a   _____
4 n u t y c r o   _____
5 p h i - o h p   _____
6 n i L t a   _____
7 z j a z   _____
8 e n c a d   _____

B Write the name of the type of music under the pictures. Use words from Exercise A.

_____   _____   _____

2 GRAMMAR: present perfect and simple past

A Are the sentences in the present perfect (PP) or the simple past (SP)?

1 I went to the Montreal Jazz Festival last year. _____
2 I've seen Jay-Z five times in concert. _____
3 I saw him play in New York City in 2012. _____
4 I've heard the new album, and it's really great. _____

B Read the conversation. Complete the sentences using the present perfect or the simple past and the verbs in parentheses.

A: **(1)** Have you ever *played* (play) in a band?
B: Yes, I **(2)** _____. I **(3)** _____ (play) in a band when I was in high school.
A: Cool. **(4)** _____ you _____ (enjoy) it?
B: Yes, I **(5)** _____. We **(6)** _____ (win) a lot of competitions.
A: And **(7)** _____ you ever _____ (be) to a music festival?
B: Yes, I **(8)** _____. I **(9)** _____ (go) to Coachella in California in 2013. It **(10)** _____ (be) fantastic.

WATCH OUT!

✗ I have never wrote a song.
✓ _____

C Complete the email with the present perfect or the simple past of verbs in the box.

| be buy do go listen play see (x2) take |

To: rbarker@mymail.mac.wd   **From:** tinas139@mymail.mac.wd
Subject: Kanye West!!!

Hi Ronnie!
Guess what? I **(1)** _____ to see Kanye West last weekend.
(2) _____ you ever _____ him in concert?
I **(3)** _____ him three times, but he **(4)** _____ never
_____ in our city before. A lot of people **(5)** _____ at the
concert. I **(6)** _____ some pictures (see attachment). I **(7)** _____
his new CD after the concert, and I **(8)** _____ to it all day yesterday. It's
amazing! What **(9)** _____ you _____ last weekend?
Love,
Tina

A Look at the picture and the headline in the article. Answer these questions before you read the article.

1 The music on this album is …
   a) unusual.   **b)** traditional.   **c)** electronic.
2 This album is …
   a) heavy metal.   **b)** country.   **c)** fusion.

MUSIC NEWS   New album explores jazz, blues, and soul

Radio Music Society is the fourth album by Esperanza Spalding and her fans will not be disappointed. With energy and charm, Spalding creates a melodic journey that explores a fusion of jazz, blues, and soul. Pop music and jazz music fans alike will be pleasantly surprised by her original new songs as well as new musical interpretations of classics.

Originally from Portland, Oregon, Spalding first taught herself to play the violin at the age of five, but has played the double bass since she was 14. In 2011, she was the first jazz artist to win the GRAMMY Award for Best New Artist. As well as experimenting with old and new forms of musical styles, the album is a celebration of the many types of music that have influenced her and inspired her own musical journey.

"I love this album! I listened to it in the car this morning and now I can't stop playing it!" *Molly, Seattle*

"I don't like jazz, but I bought the album because of the cover. I've listened to it ten times already and I realized that it's one of the best albums I have ever heard!" *Rick, Toronto*

B Read the article in Exercise A to check your predictions. Then circle T (true) or F (false).

1 Spalding is a jazz musician.   T / F
2 She has always played the double bass.   T / F
3 The album won a GRAMMY Award in 2011.   T / F
4 Spalding has been influenced by many types of music.   T / F
5 Jazz fans will not like her album.   T / F
6 Rick bought the album because he likes jazz.   T / F

4 VOCABULARY: adjectives for describing music

A Match the words 1–6 to those with a similar meaning a–f.

1	happy	a)	loud
2	calm	b)	old-fashioned
3	boring	c)	catchy
4	noisy	d)	upbeat
5	not modern	e)	relaxing
6	easy to sing	f)	repetitive

B Complete the sentences with adjectives from the second column of Exercise A.

1 I can't get that song out of my head. It's really _____.
2 I can't stand heavy metal. It's very _____.
3 It's the same beat and melody over and over again. It's _____.
4 This music makes me feel great! It's really _____.
5 I love really romantic music. It's so _____.
6 In my opinion, classical music is very traditional. It's _____.

5 GRAMMAR: *should* and *ought to* for advice

A Choose the correct words to complete the sentences and questions.

1 The tickets will sell out soon. They ... buy tickets now.
  a) should   b) ought
2 The new Pink album is awesome. You ... listen to it.
  a) should   b) ought
3 ... I ask Maria to go to the concert with me?
  a) Should   b) Ought
4 You ... use my computer to download music. It's illegal!
  a) don't should   b) shouldn't
5 The concert starts in 20 minutes. We ... to leave now.
  a) should   b) ought
6 I don't have enough money to buy tickets. What ... do?
  a) I should   b) should I

B Match the problems 1–6 to the solutions a–f. Then complete the solutions with *should*, *shouldn't*, or *ought*.

1 What kind of music CD should I buy for my brother?
2 The music is too loud. It could damage your ears.
3 These concert tickets are too expensive.
4 Should I buy this album? Is this band any good?
5 My sister plays heavy metal all the time at home. I don't like it.
6 I want to learn more about jazz music.

a) You _____ search online for cheaper tickets.
b) You _____ borrow some Miles Davis CDs from the library.
c) You _____ to listen to their music on YouTube before you buy it.
d) You _____ turn the volume up so high.
e) You _____ ask him about his favorite bands.
f) You _____ to ask her to turn the volume down.

C Complete the sentences with *should/shouldn't* or *ought*.

1 **A:** _____ I buy tickets on the day of the concert? Is it a good idea?
   B: No, you _____. They're usually more expensive.

2 **A:** What kind of music _____ my friends have at their party?
   B: I think they _____ to ask the guests to bring music to the party.

3 **A:** My girlfriend bought me tickets to see a band, but I don't like them. _____ I tell her?
   B: Yes, you _____. It's best to be honsest in these situations.

6 SPEAKING: starting and ending a conversation

A ⏵🔊11 **Listen to the conversations. Match the conversation starters to the correct responses. Then listen and check your answers.**

1 Hi. Great music!
2 Are you enjoying the concert?
3 So, have you seen this band before?
4 Excuse me. Do you know anything about this album?

a) Yes, I downloaded it last week. It's really catchy!
b) Yes, this music is great for dancing.
c) It's cool! This band is so good live.
d) Yes, I have. I saw them last year. You should buy their album.

B ⏵🔊12 **Listen to the conversations. Are the people starting or ending a conversation? Choose the correct option.**

Conversation 1:
a) starting a conversation   b) ending a conversation
Conversation 2:
a) starting a conversation   b) ending a conversation
Conversation 3:
a) starting a conversation   b) ending a conversation
Conversation 4:
a) starting a conversation   b) ending a conversation

Listen and write

A  13 Listen to three people talking about what kind of music they like. Complete the table.

Adele

Björk

Angélique Kidjo

	Tania	Nick	Chris
Favorite kind of music			
Favorite musician or singer	Name: Country:	Name: Country:	Name: Country:
Why do they like this musician or singer?			

B Complete the table with information about your favorite music.

Favorite kind of music	
Favorite musicians, singers, or bands	
Why do you like this singer/ musician/band?	

Over to You

C ✎ Write a paragraph in your notebook about your favorite music. Use your information from the table in Exercise B and the sentences in the Writing tutor to help you start.

DOWN TIME

Placido Domingo

Billie Holiday

A   Test your music knowledge.

1   Placido Domingo is a famous singer of which kind of music?
☐ jazz   ☐ opera   ☐ rock

2   Carnegie Hall is a famous concert hall in which city?
☐ New York   ☐ London   ☐ Paris

3   Which city in the U.S.A. is famous for jazz music?
☐ Chicago   ☐ San Francisco ☐ New Orleans

4   Paul McCartney was a member of which band?
☐ The Beatles   ☐ The Rolling Stones   ☐ The Doors

5   When did rap music first become popular?
☐ 1950s   ☐ 1970s   ☐ 1980s

6   Billie Holiday was a popular singer of which kind of music?
☐ rock   ☐ jazz   ☐ folk

7   Which famous awards are given to the best musicians every year?
☐ GRAMMY   ☐ Oscar®   ☐ Nobel

8   Who sang with *The Wailers*?
☐ Elvis Presley ☐ Bob Marley   ☐ David Bowie

9   Beyoncé was a member of which girl band?
☐ The Spice Girls   ☐ The Pussycat Dolls   ☐ Destiny's Child

10 Who composed the theme song for the 2012 James Bond movie *Skyfall*?
☐ Madonna   ☐ Alicia Keys   ☐ Adele

7–10   Your knowledge of music is excellent.
4–6   Your knowledge of music is average.
0–3   You need to explore new musical directions.

B   Find five words connected to music.
The words can go forward (→) or down (↓).

C	O	N	C	E	R	T	W	V	C
Z	A	H	N	D	G	U	L	G	O
J	A	Z	B	V	V	J	S	O	U
C	L	A	S	S	I	C	A	L	N
S	F	R	R	G	K	E	D	I	T
D	U	J	E	C	O	L	P	Z	R
J	S	R	O	P	D	S	J	S	Y
A	I	R	Q	E	E	B	P	P	F
Z	O	K	S	W	V	P	H	E	H
Z	N	N	M	U	B	L	A	Z	L

UNIT 6 LIVING SPACES

1 VOCABULARY: objects in a house

A Write words for at least three objects in each of the rooms. Check the spelling in your Student's Book or a dictionary.

B 🎧 14 Listen to a real estate agent showing a client around a house. Check the objects they mention. Then listen again and write any other objects they mention.

- ☐ nightstand
- ☐ stove
- ☐ bathtub
- ☐ dresser
- ☐ toilet
- ☐ bed
- ☐ coffee table
- ☐ sofa
- ☐ TV
- ☐ cabinets
- ☐ shower

2 GRAMMAR: *have to* for obligation and *need to* for necessity

A Complete the email with *have to / don't have to* or *need to / don't need to*.

> Hi Alexa,
>
> Thanks so much for taking care of the house while I'm away. Please remember that you **(1)** _____ feed the cat every morning and evening. And you **(2)** _____ turn off the lights in the morning, and turn them back on again at night. You **(3)** _____ water the garden because we've had so much rain recently, and you really **(4)** _____ clean the kitchen. I'll do that when I come back. You **(5)** _____ call me, but please send me an email to say everything's OK.
>
> Thanks!
>
> Elisa

B Choose the correct verb to complete each sentence.

1 You have to / don't have to put your recyclables in a recycle container.
2 You need to / don't need to separate paper and plastic.
3 You don't have to / have to put your recycling container outside your house every Monday.

C Complete the instructions for painting a house. Use the correct verb of obligation or necessity.

Painting the outside of a house looks easy, but it's very hard work. First, you **(1)** _____ clean the walls and windows. The walls **(2)** _____ be clean before you start. Next, you **(3)** _____ take off the old paint. You can't paint over the old paint. The weather is very important, too. It **(4)** _____ be sunny, but you shouldn't paint if it is rainy or humid. Finally, you **(5)** _____ use at least two coats of paint. The paint **(6)** _____ be dry before you paint over it.

Recycling your trash – dos and don'ts
Recycle container collection every Monday.

WATCH OUT!

✗ We must to call the energy company.

✓ _____

A 🎧 **15** Listen to an expert giving advice for creating more space in a home. How many main steps does she mention?

B Listen again and number the instructions in the order the expert mentions them.

- ☐ Organize your shelves.
- ☐ Sort clothes into three bags.
- ☐ Hang things up on hooks.
- ☐ Empty your closets.
- ☐ Throw away old clothes.
- ☐ Use boxes to organize small objects.
- ☐ Store winter clothing in summer.

A Complete the table.

Adjective	Adverb	Comparative adverb	Superlative adverb
slow	*slowly*	*more slowly*	*the most slowly*
careful			
fast			
good			
bad			

B Choose the correct option to complete the paragraph.

My home office is so **(1)** messy / messily and disorganized. I can never find anything and it makes life very **(2)** stressful / stressfully. So I'm trying to organize my office space more **(3)** efficient / efficiently. If all my files are organized more **(4)** careful / carefully, then I can find everything **(5)** fast / faster and **(6)** more / most easily. Then I just need to think about the **(7)** best / better way to arrange my files and books.

5 VOCABULARY: phrasal verbs

A Complete the sentences with prepositions in the box. You can use the prepositions more than once.

away   out   up

1 Could you take _____ the trash, please?
2 Remember to clean _____ after you finish cooking, OK?
3 Did you throw _____ my old magazines?
4 You can hang _____ your coat here.
5 Please put _____ these CDs after you listen to them.
6 Could you pick _____ these old newspapers off the floor?
7 Why don't you give _____ your old clothes to charity?

B Complete the paragraph with the correct form of verbs in the box.

clean hang pick put take throw

WELCOME TO *Martha's problem page*

Dear Martha,

My roommate is very messy and it's driving me crazy! I don't know what to do! She rarely **(1)** _____ up the kitchen. I always do the dishes. I **(2)** _____ out the trash every week, but she never does it!

Our living room is a complete mess. She doesn't **(3)** _____ her clothes away when they're dry so there are piles of her laundry everywhere! She never **(4)** _____ away her old newspapers. Her papers are all over the floor, but she never **(5)** _____ them up and she never **(6)** _____ her coat up either. I have to do it for her! I've tried talking to her, but she just gets offended. Please tell me what I can do!

6 WRITING: identifying paragraph structure

Read the description. Match the topic sentences to the correct paragraphs. One sentence is not necessary.

A

There are many points to consider when making this important choice.

B

First of all, you can meet and socialize with other students more easily. If you are new to the U.S.A., for example, and don't have any friends yet, that is an important advantage. Dorms usually have several common rooms such as TV lounges, social areas, shared kitchens, and laundry facilities, so it is easy to talk to other students. Another advantage is that dorms are usually on campus or have excellent transportation to and from campus, so getting back late at night is not a problem. Because there are always other people around, it also feels safer and more secure.

C

In some cases, it can be slightly cheaper, especially if you share a rented house with three or four other students. If you have some good friends that you get along well with, this can be a very good idea. Another advantage is that there are no rules or restrictions, so you have more freedom. One problem with a rented house or apartment is that not all landlords are good at maintaining their rental properties and when something goes wrong or gets broken, it can take a long time to get fixed.

 However, some students prefer to live off-campus in their second or third year.

 There are many advantages to living in a dorm.

 When they start college, students often have to choose between living in a dorm or living in a rented house.

 It is difficult to get into dorms because they are usually overbooked.

Read and write

A   **Read the descriptions. Match the questions to the correct paragraphs.**

A

I live in an apartment in Boston. It's a small apartment building. There are five floors, and I live on the third floor. My apartment has four rooms: a bedroom, a bathroom, a living room, and a kitchen. The walls are white and yellow with bright curtains and furniture. The living room has a view of a park on the opposite side of the street. It's in a very nice area with a lot of trees and green spaces around, and it's not far from the train station.

B

Living in an apartment has some disadvantages. First, it is pretty small compared to a house. I don't have space for a lot of books and clothes. Second, there isn't a yard, so I can't grow vegetables outdoors or sit outside to relax. Finally, there are some rules and restrictions for all the residents. I can't have a pet dog, for example, although cats are OK.

C

On the whole, I find that living in an apartment has many advantages. One advantage is that apartments are easier to take care of. The heat and electricity bills are usually cheaper and there's no yard work to do. Another advantage is that there are always neighbors nearby who can take care of your apartment when you are away. Finally, living in an apartment means that I can live downtown, so I am not far from the theaters, museums, and art galleries, and can enjoy all the cultural opportunities of living in Boston.

- ☐ Why do you like your home?
- ☐ What are some problems?
- ☐ What's your home like?

B   **Describe your home (or a place where you would like to live).**

- Where is it? (In a large town or city or in the country?) _____
- What kind of building is it? (A house or an apartment? How many floors?)

  _____

- What kind of furniture and colors are there? _____
- Why do you like it? _____
- What are some disadvantages? _____

Over to You

C   ✍ **Use the ideas from Exercise B to write three paragraphs in your notebook about your home.**

DOWN TIME

A Write the correct letter of each object and find the secret message.

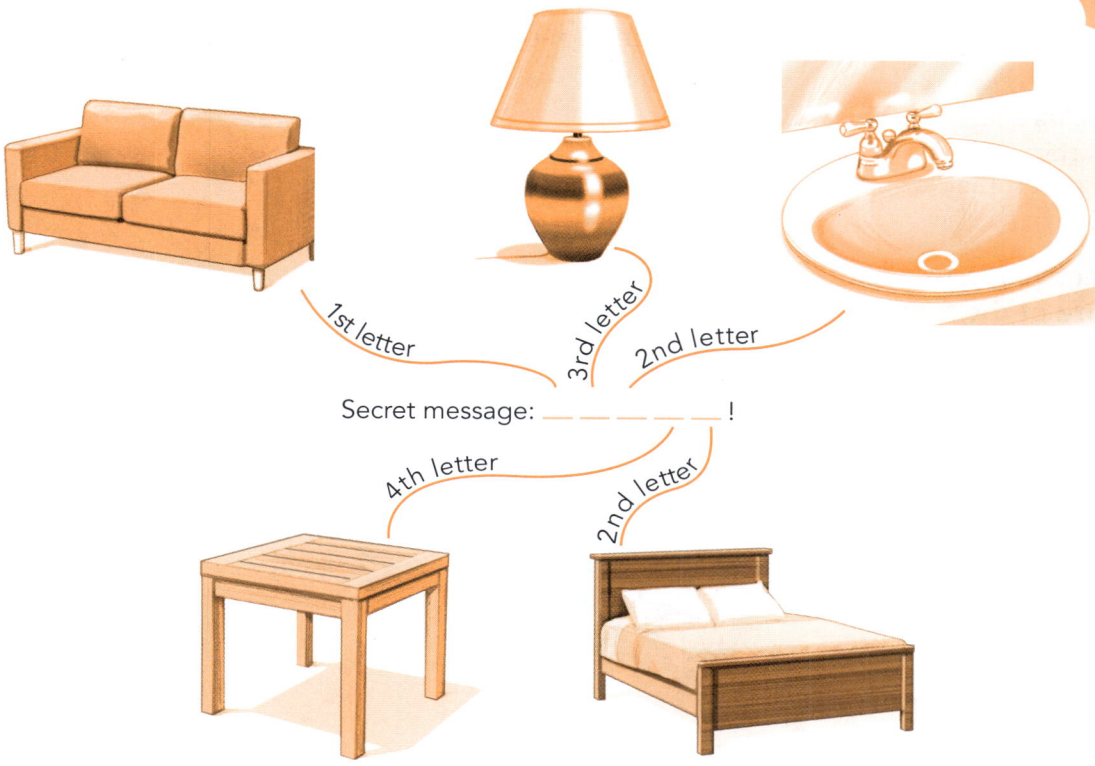

1st letter

3rd letter

2nd letter

Secret message: _ _ _ _ _ _ _ !

4th letter

2nd letter

B Find eight differences between the pictures. Write sentences in your notebook to describe them.

A

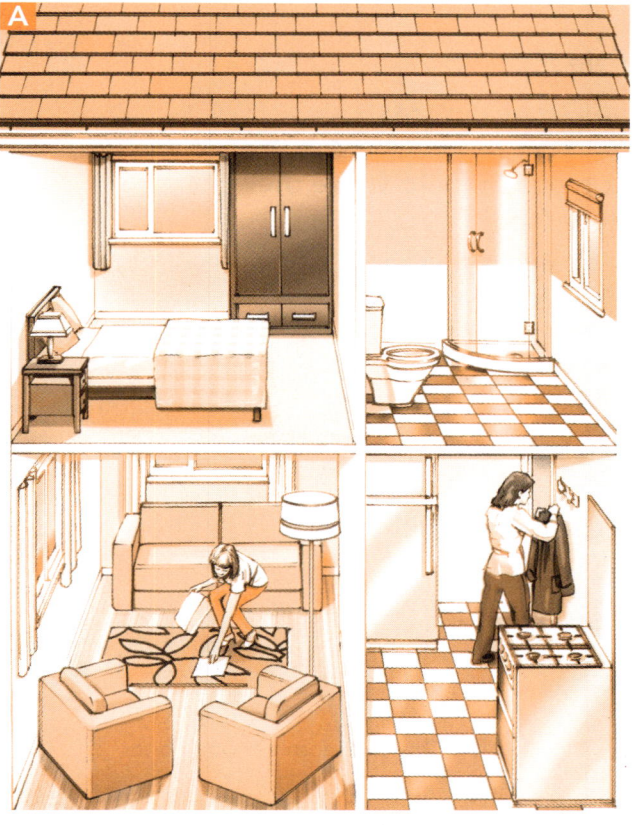

B

UNIT 7 A QUESTION OF TASTE

1 VOCABULARY: adjectives to describe food

A Complete the sentences with words to describe taste or texture.

1 Sugar isn't sour. It's _____.
2 Soy sauce isn't spicy. It's _____.
3 Lemons aren't sweet. They're _____.
4 Crackers aren't creamy. They're _____.

B Choose adjectives in the box to best describe the taste and texture of the food items.

| creamy | crunchy | greasy | juicy | salty | sour | spicy | sweet |

1 apple   *crunchy* _____   5 ginger   _____
2 mango   _____   6 potato chips   _____
3 cheese   _____   7 grapefruit   _____
4 mustard   _____   8 ice cream   _____

C 🎧 16 Listen to these people tasting different types of food. Write the words that describe each food. What is the mystery food?

1 Description _____   Mystery food _____
2 Description _____   Mystery food _____
3 Description _____   Mystery food _____
4 Description _____   Mystery food _____

2 GRAMMAR: *too, enough, not … enough*

A Write the words in the correct order to make sentences.

1 creamy / enough / not / the / dessert / is / .

_____

2 is / the / sauce / spicy / too / .

_____

3 not / toast / is / crunchy / enough / the / .

_____

4 the / ice cream / sweet / is / too / .

_____

> **WATCH OUT!**
> ✗ This coffee isn't enough hot.
> ✓ _____

B Rewrite the sentences using *too*, *enough*, or *not ... enough* and the adjective in parentheses.

1 This soup isn't hot enough. This *soup is too cold*. (*cold*)
2 This sauce doesn't need any more salt. This _____. (*salty*)
3 These French fries have a lot of oil. These _____. (*greasy*)
4 These grapes are too sour. These _____. (*sweet*)
5 This orange is too dry. This _____. (*juicy*)
6 These vegetables are too soft. These _____. (*crunchy*)
7 This lemonade doesn't need any more sugar. This _____. (*sweet*)

3 VOCABULARY: food containers

A Label the pictures with the name of the food and the correct container in the box.

bag   bottle   box   can   jar   package

1

a box of chocolates

2

_____

3

_____

4

_____

5

_____

6

_____

B Choose the correct option to complete the phrases.

1 a ... of ketchup
   a) can   b) jar   c) bottle
2 a ... of cereal
   a) can   b) bottle   c) box
3 a ... of flour
   a) package b) can   c) bottle

4 a ... of lemonade
   a) box   b) jar   c) can
5 a ... of jam
   a) jar   b) box   c) can
6 a ... of cookies
   a) bottle   b) package c) can

C 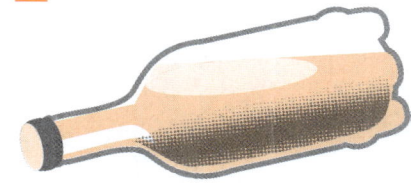 **17** Chelsea and Yuki are planning a picnic. Listen and write their shopping list.

Food for the picnic
10 bags of potato chips

4 GRAMMAR: quantifiers

A Complete the sentences with *too much*, *too many*, or *enough*.

1 You don't eat _____ vegetables. You should eat more.
2 You eat _____ potato chips. They aren't good for you.
3 Don't drink _____ lemonade. It has a lot of sugar.
4 Many people eat _____ junk food.
5 They don't eat _____ natural food.
6 I eat _____ cookies. They're not healthy!

B Read about these people's intentions to improve their diet. Complete the sentences with *less* or *fewer*.

Health and Mind Magazine

Five tips for a perfect diet

Here's what some of our readers are doing to improve their diets:

1 I want to lose weight, so I'm trying to eat _____ fried food and _____ fat, salt, and sugar.

2 Giving up cookies and chocolate is impossible! But at least I'm eating _____ cookies and _____ chocolate now.

3 I try to use _____ oil when I fry vegetables.

4 I'm trying to drink _____ cups of coffee—just one or two a day.

5 I'm going to eat _____ ice cream.

C Look at the picture and complete the note telling Harry what he needs to buy using quantifiers.

Hi Harry,
There isn't (1) _____ cheese and there's only a (2) _____ milk left. We only have a (3) _____ apples, and we definitely need (4) _____ grapes – there aren't (5) _____ at all! We have a (6) _____ of salad, though, so don't buy anymore of that. Thanks!
Fiona

WATCH OUT!

✗ I don't drink many tea.

✓ _____

5 SPEAKING explaining what you mean

Match the descriptions 1–4 to the pictures A–D.

A ☐ 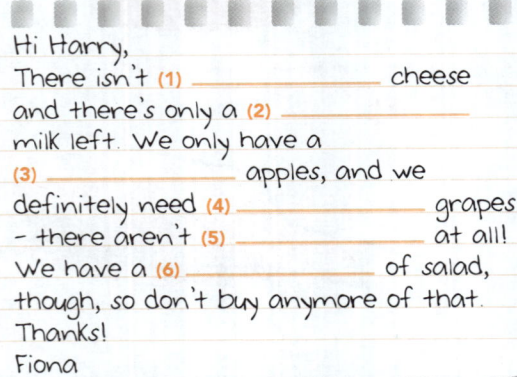 B ☐ C ☐  D ☐

avocado   pomegranate   sushi   sweet potato

1 It's a type of fruit. It looks like an apple. It's red and yellow on the outside, and inside it has a lot of juicy seeds.
2 It's green. It's like a pear, but it isn't sweet. You can prepare it with salt and lemon juice.
3 It's like a potato, but it's orange. You can fry it in butter or bake it in the oven.
4 It's a kind of Japanese food. It's made with rice and seaweed, and it usually has fish or vegetables inside it.

6 READING: prediction

A Look at the title of the article and the picture in Exercise B. What do you think the article is about?

I think the article is about _____.

B Read the first paragraph of the article. Choose one option to predict the topic of the next paragraph. Then read the next paragraph to check. Continue in the same way with paragraphs two and three.

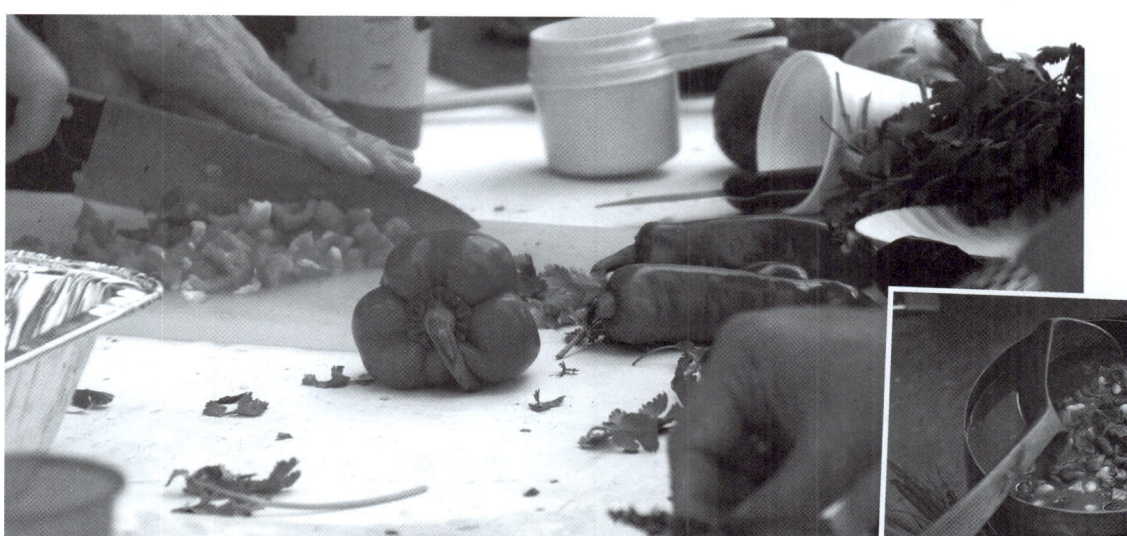

Chili cook-off

A chili cook-off is a popular social event in many cities and towns around the U.S.A. It's a competition to see who can make the best chili! A chili cook-off is a fun way to meet people, eat good food, and raise money for charity.

1 I think the topic of the next paragraph is going to be …
   a) the rules of a chili cook-off
   b) how to choose the best chili

A chili cook-off has a number of different rules. Visitors buy a button (the money goes to prizes and to charity). Each chef's name is a secret (so you can't vote for your friends). The visitors taste each dish and vote. Sometimes there are several prizes. For example, the most traditional, the most creative, or the spiciest chili. Anyone can enter the competition with their favorite chili recipe.

2 I think the topic of the next paragraph is going to be …
   a) types of chili dishes
   b) reasons to eat chili

The basic ingredients are onions, garlic, and, of course, chili peppers. Some people cook chili with beef, tomatoes, and beans. Others prefer a vegetarian version and add other vegetables such as green peppers and corn. Some like chili that is very spicy and hot. They include extra hot chilis as well as a lot of paprika. Every chef tries to have the best and most original recipe to win the cook-off.

C Now read the whole article again and choose the correct answers.

1 What is a *cook-off*?   a party / a competition / a national holiday
2 Who decides the winner of the cook-off?   friends / chefs / visitors
3 Does everyone have to use the same recipe?   yes / no / doesn't say

Listen and write

A 🔊 **18** Listen to three people talking about the most unusual food they have ever tasted. Match the pictures to the speakers.

A – peanut butter and jam sandwich ☐

B – pickled herring on toast ☐

C – crocodile ☐

B Listen again and use key words to complete the table.

	Where did they eat it?	How do they describe it?	Did they like it?
1			
2			
3			

C Think about the most unusual food you have ever tried. Answer the questions.

1 What did you eat?

2 Where did you eat it?

3 What did it look/smell/taste/feel like?

4 Did you enjoy it?

Over to You

D ✏️ Use your answers from Exercise C to write a paragraph in your notebook about your unusual food experience.

DOWN TIME

Food of the **World**

A Choose the one that doesn't belong.

1	Which food is not a fruit?	shrimp	banana	apple	orange
2	Which food is not made from milk?	cheese	yogurt	pasta	butter
3	Which one is not a fish?	tuna	salmon	herring	turkey
4	Which one is not vegetarian?	beans	steak	ketchup	spaghetti

B Choose the correct answer.

1 What kind of food do people eat in China to celebrate the New Year?
   a) eggs　　　　　b) noodles　　　　c) carrots

2 What kind of food do people eat in the U.S.A. at Thanksgiving?
   a) turkey　　　　b) beef　　　　　c) fish

3 On New Year's Eve in Spain, people eat …
   a) watermelon.　b) oranges.　　　c) grapes.

4 People in England eat Yorkshire pudding together with …
   a) beef.　　　　b) toast.　　　　c) cream.

5 What kind of food is caviar?
   a) frogs' legs　　b) sharks' teeth　c) fish eggs

6 Parmesan is a type of cheese made in …
   a) Canada.　　　b) France.　　　c) Italy.

7 Sushi is a kind of Japanese food made from fish and …
   a) noodles.　　　b) rice.　　　　c) bread.

8 In Japan, people often eat steamed rice with a pickled …
   a) cherry.　　　b) lemon.　　　　c) plum.

9 In Mexico, a special sauce for chicken called "mole" is made with …
   a) chocolate.　　b) seafood.　　　c) curry.

10 Chili is a kind of spicy stew made from meat, chili peppers, garlic, and …
   a) oranges.　　　b) onions.　　　c) broccoli.

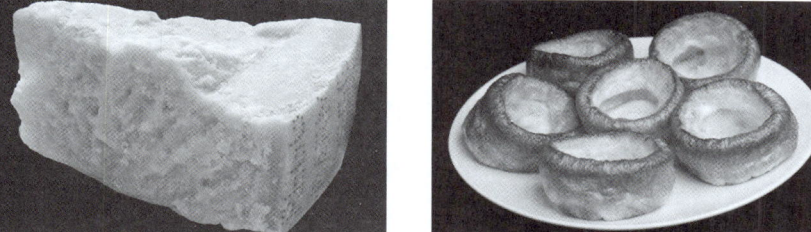

UNIT 8 LOVE AND ROMANCE

1 VOCABULARY: relationships

A Match the sentences A–E to the descriptions 1–5.

A We're going to get married!

D I'll wear a red scarf so you'll recognize me.

B Will you have dinner with me?

E This is my girlfriend.

C I don't want to see you anymore!

1 ☐ He's asking her out.
2 ☐ They're breaking up.
3 ☐ They're going out with each other.
4 ☐ They got engaged.
5 ☐ She's going on a blind date.

B 🎧 19 **Complete the conversation. Then listen and check your answers.**

A: Have Mike and Rachel **(1)** _____? I haven't seen them together recently.

B: Yes, Mike's **(2)** _____ with Julianna now. I think they just
(3) _____.

A: Really? They haven't known each other that long, right?

B: No, they met on a **(4)** _____ about a month ago. The next day, he
(5) _____ her _____ again, and the rest is history.

A: That's great news! I hope they'll be happy!

2 GRAMMAR: expressing likes, desires, and preferences

A **Choose the correct option.**

1 Would you like see / to see a movie tomorrow?
2 I'd rather not eat / to eat dinner too early.
3 Do you like cook / cooking Italian food?
4 Would you prefer go out / to go out to a restaurant or stay at home?
5 I'd like go / to go to a party this weekend.
6 Would you rather have / to have Mexican or Indian food tonight?
7 We'd prefer cook / to cook dinner at home.
8 Kyla likes watching / watch action movies.

B **Write the words in the correct order to make sentences.**

1 I / to / go / would / like / to / a party / .

_____

2 for / would / like / you / to / go / dinner / out / ?

_____

3 would / tonight / not / go / rather / we / out / .

_____

4 home / prefer / you / would / to / eat / at / ?

_____

5 not / eat / prefer / Italian / would / to / food / I / .

_____

6 go / would / rather / you / a movie / to / ?

_____

WATCH OUT!

 I'd rather not to see a movie tonight.

✓ _____

C What would you like to do on your first date? Write questions using the prompts. Then write true answers.

1 prefer / go to a movie
   A: *Would you prefer to go to a movie?*
   B: *No, I wouldn't.*

2 prefer / talk in a café
   A: _____
   B: _____

3 rather / meet with a group of friends
   A: _____
   B: _____

4 rather / go dancing
   A: _____
   B: _____

5 prefer / talk about music
   A: _____
   B: _____

6 would like / have dinner with your parents
   A: _____
   B: _____

3 GRAMMAR: gerund phrases as subject and object

A Underline the gerund in each sentence. Then check the correct option.

	Subject	Object	After a preposition
1 I'm thinking of having a party.	☐	☐	☐
2 Going to parties alone is pretty hard.	☐	☐	☐
3 I love dancing and listening to music.	☐	☐	☐
4 I'm good at talking to people at parties.	☐	☐	☐
5 I hate giving parties.	☐	☐	☐
6 Playing loud music at a party isn't a good idea.	☐	☐	☐

B Complete the paragraph with the gerund form of the verbs in the box.

ask   chat   date   fill   get   give   go (x2)   make   meet

Online dating is the perfect way to meet your ideal partner. **(1)** _____ out the registration is fast and easy—and best of all it's completely free. **(2)** _____ us details of your age, job, and interests will help us to search our database and find the perfect partner for you. It's easier than **(3)** _____ on a blind date. It's easier than **(4)** _____ someone out for the first time. **(5)** _____ to know a person online is a great way to find out if you are a perfect match! Most people are nervous about **(6)** _____ on their first date. **(7)** _____ online by text message or webcam before you meet are much better ideas! Our online service makes **(8)** _____ easy and fun! **(9)** _____ people and **(10)** _____ friends has never been easier!

WATCH OUT!

✗ I really enjoy go to parties.

✓ _____

C Rewrite these sentences using a gerund.

1 It is easy to meet people at parties.
_____ is easy.

2 It is fun to have dinner with friends.
_____ is fun.

3 I feel sad when I argue with friends.
I don't like _____.

4 I feel upset when I'm late for a meeting.
I hate _____.

5 I never go out alone at night because I'm afraid.
I'm afraid of _____.

6 He doesn't want to get engaged because he's nervous.
He's nervous about _____.

4 WRITING: identifying paragraph structure

The sentences from two paragraphs are mixed up. Identify the sentences that go with each topic sentence. Write the sentence letters in the correct order below each topic sentence.

Topic sentence Paragraph 1: Hummingbird mating season begins around the end of March in North America.

_____
_____
_____

Topic sentence Paragraph 2: When the female hummingbirds arrive a few days later, the males begin trying to attract a mate.

_____
_____
_____

a) Males usually fly there from Mexico or Cental America before the females.
b) It's important for the male to establish his territory around their mating place and guard it against intruders.
c) Other strategies include singing and flapping their wings as fast as possible to create a loud humming sound.
d) As soon as they arrive, they begin to look for a mating place.
e) The males fly high up into the air, and then dive straight down back toward the ground again.
f) The most important method of attracting the females is to fly around energetically.

5 LISTENING: understanding instructions and processes

A **You are going to listen to a lecture about the Eastern Brown Pelican. First, read these statements and circle T (true) or F (false).**

1. Pelicans reproduce once a year.   T / F
2. The female lays only one egg.   T / F
3. Male and female pelicans build nests together.   T / F
4. Male pelicans do not incubate the eggs.   T / F
5. Baby pelicans can talk to their parents from inside the egg.   T / F
6. Only female pelicans can feed the babies.   T / F

B 🎧 **20 Now listen to the lecture and check your answers to Exercise A.**

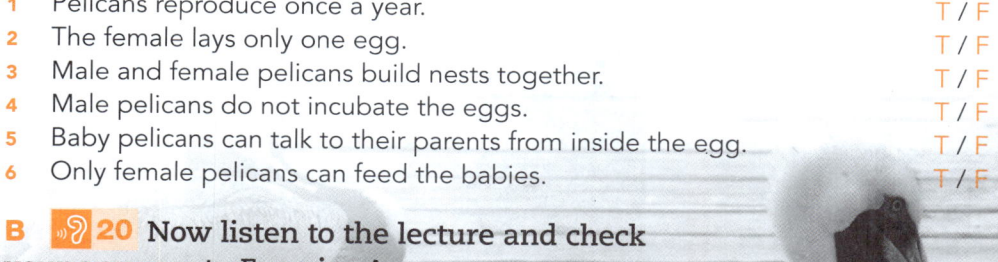

6 VOCABULARY: *get* + adjective

A **Match the situations 1–6 to the consequences a–f.**

1. Manuel got lost and couldn't find his friends.
2. Pete ate some uncooked chicken.
3. Martina broke her favorite vase.
4. Henry had nothing to do.
5. Yukiko had nothing to drink.
6. Adele ran a marathon.

a) She got angry.
b) He got bored.
c) He got worried.
d) She got thirsty.
e) She got tired.
f) He got sick.

B **Complete the conversations with questions. Use *get* and a word in the box.**

| angry   better   ~~hungry~~   sick   thirsty   tired |

1. **A:** We forgot to take food with us on our trip.
   B: *Did you get hungry?*

2. **A:** We spent eight hours hiking up a mountain.
   B: _____

3. **A:** I forgot my boyfriend's birthday.
   B: _____

4. **A:** We ate some berries and plants, but they weren't good.
   B: _____

5. **A:** My son had a bad cold and had to stay at home for four days.
   B: _____

6. **A:** We went bike riding, but left our water bottles at home.
   B: _____

Read and write

A Read these people's descriptions of their first date. Then complete the table.

> On my first date, I went to a Chinese restaurant with a boy from school, and we ate noodles. I remember it was kind of hard to eat them with chopsticks, so I got shy and nervous, and only ate half of the food. He didn't seem to mind though, and afterward he asked me out again. I said yes, but on a first date, I'd prefer to eat Mexican food or pizza. (Gloria)

> I went on a blind date with a friend of my sister. We went bowling and I got bored, and I think she did, too. We didn't go on any more dates together after that. I'd rather go to a concert for a first date. (Takeo)

	What did they do on their first date?	How did they feel?	What would they prefer to do on a first date?
Gloria			
Takeo			

B Make notes about the first time you did something (your first date, your first driving lesson, your first visit to a foreign country…).

What did you do?	How did you feel?	Was it a good experience? Why or why not?

Over to You

C Use your notes in Exercise B to write a paragraph in your notebook about your experience.

WRITING TUTOR

I'll always remember the first time I …
I have never forgotten the first time I …
The first time I … was when I …
… was one of the best experiences of my life.

DOWN TIME

A Write a sentence below each picture of a stage in Tim and Sue's relationship. Then number them in the correct order.

☐ _____

☐ _____

☐ _____

☐ _____

☐ _____

☐ _____

B Read the clues. Complete the puzzle. Unscramble the letters. What's the mystery word?

1 I don't have any food. I'm _____.
2 I don't have any water. I'm _____.
3 The bus is late! I'm _____.
4 There's nothing on TV! I'm _____.
5 I was sick, but now I'm _____.
6 There's a spider! I'm _____.
7 We were engaged, and now we're _____.

Mystery word: _ _ _ _ _ _ _

UNIT 9 OUR PLANET

1 VOCABULARY: the weather

A Complete the sentences with words in the box.

foggy rains snows stormy sunny windy

1 We usually go skiing when it _____.
2 The best time to fly a kite is when it is _____.
3 It's nice to sit on the beach when it is _____.
4 Sometimes there is thunder and lightning when it is _____.
5 You should drive carefully when it is very _____.
6 It's not much fun playing soccer when it _____.

B 🎧 21 Listen to the conversations. Write the weather words you hear.

Conversation 1:
_____

Conversation 3:
_____

Conversation 2:
_____

Conversation 4:
_____

C Choose the correct option to complete the sentences.

1 Look at the snow / snowy outside!
2 It isn't rain / raining right now.
3 It will be storm / stormy tomorrow.
4 Listen to the wind / windy!
5 Does it rain / rainy a lot in your country?
6 It's very cloud / cloudy today.

2 GRAMMAR: *may, might,* and *will* for future possibility

A Choose the correct option to complete the sentences.

1 I'm sure you may / will have a good time at the concert.
2 I'm not sure, but I may / will be home early tonight.
3 We might / will definitely meet again.
4 They might / will go on vacation this year, but they haven't planned it yet.
5 Are you sure it may / will rain tomorrow?
6 We don't know yet, but it might / will be very cold tonight.

B There is one mistake in each sentence. Find and correct it.

1 We might to go swimming this weekend.

_____

2 I'm sure it willn't rain today.

_____

3 We may to get a lot of snow this winter.

_____

4 I may definitely go to the beach next weekend.

_____

5 They not might go on vacation this year.

_____

6 It will be probably sunny tomorrow.

_____

C Make sentences about the pictures. Use *may*, *might*, or *will*.
More than one answer is possible.

1 **a)** not find a new job (*not sure*)
  b) get some good advice (*sure*)

2 **a)** go into the store (*sure*)
  b) buy a new dress (*not sure*)

3 **a)** not finish her work today (*sure*)
  b) be very tired when she goes home (*not sure*)

1 **a)** *He may/might not find a new job.*
  b) _____
3 **a)** _____
  b) _____

2 **a)** _____
  b) _____

3 SPEAKING: interrupting

A Write the words in the correct order to make ways of interrupting.

1 me / excuse / for / I / interrupt / you / a / can / second / ?
  Excuse me, _____

2 ask / question / quick / can / I / a / me / excuse / ?
  _____

3 interrupt / sorry / what / the / homework / was / to / but / ?
  _____

B 🎧 **22** Listen to the conversations. Use key words to complete the table.

	What is the topic of the main conversation?	Reason for interrupting
Conversation 1		
Conversation 2		
Conversation 3		

4 VOCABULARY: the natural world

A Label the map with the names of the natural features in the box.

field   forest   hill   island   lake   mountain   river   sea

B Complete the descriptions with words from Exercise A.

1. Australia is the largest _____ in the world.
2. Baikal is a large _____ in central Russia.
3. Everest is the highest _____ in the Himalayas.
4. The Mediterranean is the _____ between Europe and North Africa.
5. The Nile is a _____ that runs through Egypt.
6. The Amazon is a large tropical _____ in South America.

(1) _____
(2) _____
(3) _____
(4) _____
(5) _____
(6) _____
(7) _____
(8) _____

5 READING: understanding meaning from context

A Quickly read this article, ignoring any words or phrases you don't know. Then read the sentences and circle T (true) or F (false).

The Amazon Rain forest

The Amazon Rain forest is located in South America near the equator. The forest covers several countries including Brazil, Peru, and Colombia. It is the largest rain forest in the world and is home to millions of different animal and insect species, as well as over 40,000 plant species. These include many **unknown** plants and animals that may be useful in research for new medicines.

Some environmentalists predict that the rain forest may not **survive** for much longer. The main problem is **deforestation**. Farmers are cutting down trees to make farms and fields. People are also cutting down trees to build homes. Global warming is a problem, too. Some experts suggest that a rise in world temperatures might **destroy** around 75% of the Amazon Rain forest. If this happens, many plants and animals will lose their natural **habitat**, and we will lose an important part of our planet's ecosystem.

1. The Amazon Rain forest is larger than other forests. T / F
2. Millions of animals live in the Amazon Rain forest. T / F
3. Farms help to protect the rain forest. T / F
4. Climate change will affect the Amazon Rain forest. T / F

B Read the article again and look at the words in bold. Look at the context carefully and choose the correct meaning.

1 unknown a) natural b) new
2 survive a) continue to live b) get bigger
3 deforestation a) losing trees b) planting trees
4 destroy a) improve b) kill
5 habitat a) home b) climate

6 GRAMMAR: *will* and *going to*

A Match the sentences 1–6 to the correct description a–c.

1 [c] I'll take you on a trip to the mountains.
2 ☐ I'm going to help clean up the beach this weekend.
3 ☐ Climate change will continue to cause floods.
4 ☐ We're going to hike in the forest next week.
5 ☐ Many regions are going to have a lot of rain this year.
6 ☐ I'll try to do more to stop climate change.

a) make a prediction about the future
b) talk about future plans and intentions
c) make spontanious offers and decisions

B How do you think climate change will affect us in the future? Complete the sentences with *will* or *won't*.

1 Pollution _____ get worse.
2 The earth's climate _____ get warmer.
3 The global population _____ increase.
4 Some countries _____ have enough food.
5 Some animal species _____ survive.
6 Icebergs _____ melt.

C 🎧 23 Complete the conversations with the correct form of *will* or *going to* and the verb in parentheses. Then listen and check your answers.

Conversation 1
A: What **(1)** _____ you _____ (*do*) to help the environment?
B: I **(2)** _____ (*not drive*) my car when I can use public transportation. What about you?
A: We **(3)** _____ (*save*) electricity by using solar panels on our house.
B: That's a good idea! **(4)** _____ there _____ (*be*) enough sunshine?
A: Well, there **(5)** _____ (*not be*) as much sunshine in the winter, but there should be enough daylight.

Conversation 2
A: I **(6)** _____ (*join*) this new climate change organization.
B: Really? What **(7)** _____ they _____ (*do*) to stop climate change?
A: They **(8)** _____ (*make*) simple changes. For example, I **(9)** _____ (*ride*) my bike to work, and I **(10)** _____ (*not use*) plastic bags.
B: That's a good idea! Maybe I **(11)** _____ (*do*) that, too!

Listen and write

A Look at the pictures. In which place would you like to live?

B 🎧 **24** Listen to three people talking about their ideal place to live.
Match each person to the correct picture in Exercise A.

Person 1: _____

Person 2: _____

Person 3: _____

C Listen again and take notes.

	1	2	3
Country / City			
Natural features / Climate			
Advantages			
Disadvantages			
Lifestyle activities			

D What is your ideal place to live? Choose one place in the world and
describe it. Make notes.

Kind of place (e.g., town, village, island, etc.)	
Natural features / Climate	
Advantages / Disadvantages	
Lifestyle activities	

Over to You

E ✏️ Use your notes from Exercise D to write a paragraph
in your notebook about your ideal place to live and
explain why.

WRITING TUTOR

*My ideal place to live is …
My dream home is in/on/near a …
Some people might want to live
in/on/near a … , but I'm going to
live in/on/near a …*

DOWN TIME

A **Choose the one that doesn't belong.**

1	island	hill	field	snow
2	rain	wind	island	fog
3	lake	mountain	sea	river
4	sunny	rain	snow	hail
5	windy	weather	rainy	foggy

B **Look at the clues and complete the crossword.**

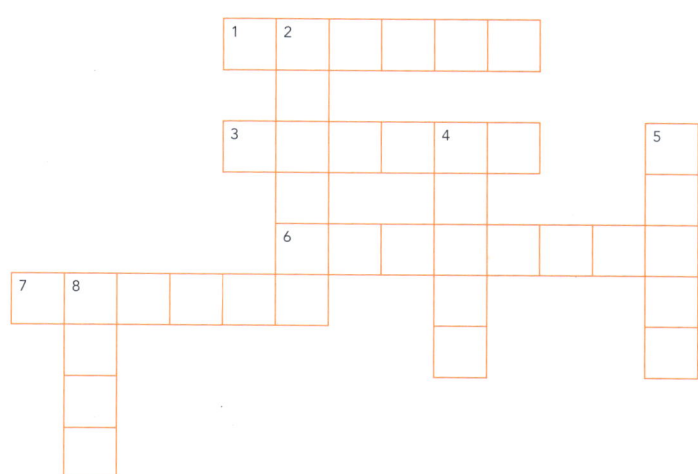

UNIT 10 PARTY ANIMALS

1 VOCABULARY: parties

A Complete the missing words.

1. h _ _ _ _ a conversation

2. give a _ _ _ _ _

3. d _ _ _ _ _ _ _ the house

4. Welcome the g _ _ _ _ _ _

5. bring some s _ _ _ _ _

6. p _ _ _ music

B Complete the paragraph with words in the box.

> conversation   decorated   gift   guests   invited   made   music   snacks

Last Saturday, we had a party for my grandfather's 70th birthday. We **(1)** _____ over 40 **(2)** _____. I prepared the **(3)** _____ and the drinks. My sister **(4)** _____ a delicious cake. It had candles on it. We **(5)** _____ the living room with balloons and paper chains. My sister's husband brought some **(6)** _____ and his guitar. We all sang *Happy Birthday* and gave Grandpa our **(7)** _____—a large photograph of the whole family. Everyone danced and talked until midnight. I had an interesting **(8)** _____ with some friends about movies and music. Grandpa said the party was awesome!

2 GRAMMAR: infinitives of purpose

A Last weekend, Marisa went to Mexico for a wedding. Complete the list of her preparations for the trip with phrases in the box and the word *to*.

> book a room   buy a new dress   buy some new shoes
> get some money   pack her bag   reserve a flight   rest

1. First, she called a hotel _____.
2. Then she went to the airline website _____.
3. Next, she went to the bank _____.
4. After that, she went to a clothes store _____.
5. Then she went to a shoe store _____.
6. Finally, she went home _____ and _____.

WATCH OUT!

✗ She went to Mexico for to see her friend.

✓ _____

B Complete the sentences with *in order to* or *in order not to* and the correct verb in the box.

> disturb help increase let make take

Rules for parties in the dorm social room

1. You can move furniture out of the living room _____ space for dancing.
2. You can put signs outside _____ guests find their way.
3. Please park cars on the side streets _____ up all the parking spaces.
4. You can open the back windows _____ in fresh air.
5. You should play music quietly _____ other students.
6. Please clear away all the trash _____ more work for the cleaning staff.

3 VOCABULARY: adjectives for describing events

A Choose the correct word to complete the sentences.

1. There were so many people. It was very crowded / empty.
2. I really enjoyed the quiet music. The atmosphere was very lively / relaxed.
3. I didn't like the food. It was great / awful.
4. A lot of people were dancing. It was very lively / relaxed.
5. The music was too loud / soft. I couldn't hear it at all.
6. I had a great time. It was really awful / fun.

B Choose words in the box to describe the two pictures.

> lively loud relaxed soft

Atmosphere: _____   Atmosphere: _____
Music: _____   Music: _____

4 WRITING: topic sentences

A Choose the best topic sentence for this paragraph.

a) There are many reasons to have a party.
b) Organizing a party can be very stressful.
c) Parties are a good way to meet people.

Many people have a party to celebrate their birthday. It's also popular to have parties when you get engaged or married. In some countries, people like to have a housewarming party to celebrate moving into a new home. A recent trend is the "painting party" where you invite friends over to paint the walls of your new home. It's fun and a great way to get some help with fixing up your new home.

B Match the topic sentences to the correct paragraph.

a) It's important to create a good atmosphere.
b) It's a good idea to prepare the food well in advance.
c) A good host makes every guest feel welcome.

TOP TIPS Party Etiquette

1 _____ When they arrive, go to the door to greet them. Shake their hands and make them feel that you are pleased to see them. Then introduce them to some of the other guests. Think of a topic they have in common and get them talking to each other before you move on. If they feel welcome, everyone will be more relaxed and ready to have a good time.

2 _____ You can use lighting to create a different mood, or move your furniture around to create more space. Decorate your room and play some music in the background because it will help people to relax.

Soft music will encourage good conversations and people will not have to shout. Put chairs around the room, but not too many. You want people to move around and not stay sitting in one place.

3 _____ Make a list of all the snacks and drinks you need, and if appropriate, ask your guests to bring something to eat and drink. Make sure you have food for vegetarians and those who are allergic to nuts or milk. Provide a variety of drinks. Make sure you have plenty of extra bread or crackers in case you run out of food at the end of the party.

5 LISTENING: understanding agreement and disagreement

A Write the expressions in the correct place in the table.

I completely agree.   I don't agree.   I don't think that's right   I'm not sure I agree.
That's not true.   Yes, that's right.   Yes, that's true.   You're absolutely right.

Strongly agree	Agree	Disagree	Strongly disagree

B **»25** Listen to the conversations and decide if the two people agree or disagree.

1 agree / disagree
2 agree / disagree
3 agree / disagree

C Listen again. Which three phrases are in the conversations? Write the number of the conversation.

☐ I completely agree.
☐ I don't agree.
☐ I'm not sure I agree.
☐ That's not true.

☐ Yes, that's right.
☐ Yes, that's true.
☐ You're absolutely right.
☐ I don't think that's right.

6 GRAMMAR: review of future forms

A Match sentences 1–6 to their meanings a–f.

1 The party starts at nine tonight.
2 We're renting a large hall for the party.
3 The weather will be fine.
4 We're going to invite all our friends.
5 I'll help you clean up after the party.
6 I'm going to have a party next week.

a) future arrangement
b) intention
c) future prediction
d) future plan
e) spontaneous decision
f) scheduled event

B Choose the correct option.

1 A: I have / am having a party on Saturday. Can you come?
   B: Sure! I'll / I'm going to come over about seven, OK?

2 A: What are you going to / will you cook for the guests?
   B: We're having / We'll have a barbecue. It's all prepared.

3 A: We're going / We'll go on vacation tomorrow.
   B: Really? Where will you / are you going to go?

4 A: Let's go! The train is leaving / leaves at six.
   B: OK. It won't take / It's not taking long to get there.

5 A: What do you do / are you doing tonight?
   B: I'm going to / I'll watch a movie on TV.

WATCH OUT!

ⓧ Do you stay at home tonight?

✓ _____

C Complete the email with the correct future form of the verb in parentheses.

Dear Carrie,

Thanks so much for your email. I'm very excited to hear about your housewarming party!
What time (1) _____ it _____ (start)? What (2) _____
you _____ (wear)? I think I (3) _____ (wear) my green silk dress.
Hopefully, we (4) _____ (have) some nice weather and we can sit outside. What
kind of food (5) _____ you _____ (make)?
(6) I _____ (bring) some cookies and some salad—is that OK? I'm sorry
that Mark (7) _____ (come). He (8) _____ (work)! He (9)
_____ (go) to an important conference on Monday. Could I ask my neighbor
Paula to come instead? I'm sure she (10) _____ (be) thrilled!
See you soon!
Love, Tina

Read and write

A Read the letters and check the party you would rather go to.

☐

Hi Lucy!

I'm planning a birthday party for next week.
Can you come? It's going to be at my house,
and I'm going to invite about 20 people. It
starts at 9 p.m. I want to have a horror
movie theme, so you could dress up as Dracula
or a vampire if you want! We're going
to decorate the house with horror movie
posters, and play loud, scary music. Could you
think of some strange and unusual foods for
us to eat?

Angie

☐

Hi Brendan!

We're having a housewarming party on Saturday.
Would you like to come? We're inviting just a
few friends, and our new neighbor is going to
play a few songs on his guitar, so it'll be a
nice, relaxed atmosphere with some fantastic
live music. Melissa is making a salad, and Jeff
is bringing the dessert. Could you bring some
lemonade and orange juice? I can come and pick
you up at your house if you want. Let me
know.

Paul

B Answer the questionnaire about your ideal party.

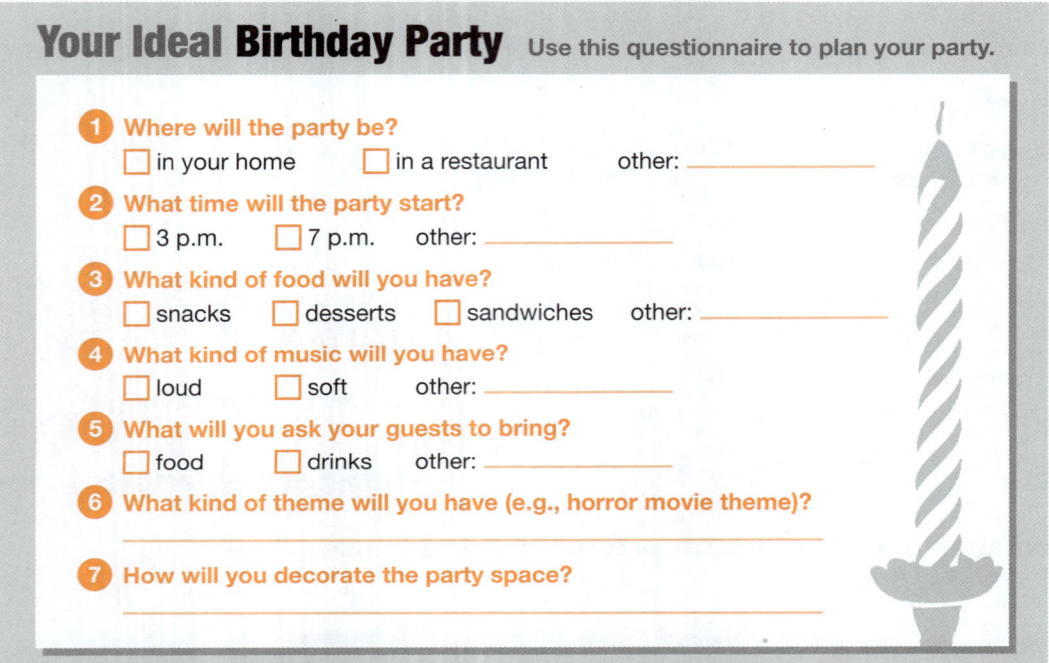

Your Ideal Birthday Party Use this questionnaire to plan your party.

1. **Where will the party be?**
   ☐ in your home ☐ in a restaurant other: _____
2. **What time will the party start?**
   ☐ 3 p.m. ☐ 7 p.m. other: _____
3. **What kind of food will you have?**
   ☐ snacks ☐ desserts ☐ sandwiches other: _____
4. **What kind of music will you have?**
   ☐ loud ☐ soft other: _____
5. **What will you ask your guests to bring?**
   ☐ food ☐ drinks other: _____
6. **What kind of theme will you have (e.g., horror movie theme)?**
   _____
7. **How will you decorate the party space?**
   _____

Over to You

C ✎ Write a letter to a friend in your notebook. Invite your friend to
the party and describe what it will be like. Use the letters in Exercise A
and the information from the questionnaire in Exercise B to help you.

DOWN TIME

A   Match the antonyms (words with the opposite meaning).

old   empty   tall
                   large
                   quiet
small   short   noisy
                   new   relaxing
crowded
                   stressful

B   Match the synonyms (words with the same meaning).

                   boring   enormous
awful
                   huge
                   lively
dull   tiny
                   noisy
loud
                   small   exciting
                   terrible

C   Read the clues. What's the mystery message?

1   The antonym of *soft*, first letter. _____
2   The synonym of *awful*, second letter. _____
3   The antonym of *crowded*, fourth letter. _____
4   Something you eat at a party, first letter. _____
5   The antonym of *sad*, first letter. _____
6   The antonym of *big*, third letter. _____
7   Exciting and active, third letter. _____
8   The synonym of *big*, last letter. _____
9   The antonym of *fantastic*, third letter. _____
10 People who go to a party, second letter. _____
11 The antonym of *quiet*, first letter. _____

Mystery message: ____ ' _____ !
                 1 2 3   4   5   6 7 8   9 10 11

UNIT 11 INNOVATE!

1 VOCABULARY: materials

A Match the materials in the box to the products.

| ceramic cotton glass metal nylon plastic rubber wood |

1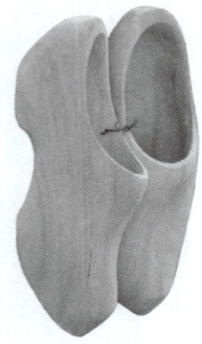

2

3

4

5

6

7

8

B What materials are these products made of? More than one answer may be possible.

1 credit card   _____
2 bench   _____
3 shopping bag   _____
4 dress   _____
5 sunglasses   _____
6 vase   _____

2 GRAMMAR: simple present passive

A Read the sentences. Are they A (active) or P (passive)?

1 These gloves are made of cotton. _____
2 We use silk and cotton to make these rugs. _____
3 They make ceramic chips in this factory. _____
4 Cotton is produced in India. _____
5 Picnic plates are made of plastic or paper. _____
6 We use nylon string for the parachutes. _____

WATCH OUT!

✗ The table is make of wood.

✓ _____

B Complete the sentences using the simple present passive of the verbs in parentheses.

1 This software *is sold* (*sell*) on the internet.
2 This product _____ (*manufacture*) in South Korea.
3 These screens _____ (*make*) from plastic.
4 Old cell phones _____ (*not recycle*).
5 _____ cars _____ (*produce*) in Mexico?
6 This camera _____ (*use*) to make videos.

C There is one mistake in each sentence. Find and correct it.

1 Plastic and glass are not recycle in my country. _____
2 Solar energy used to generate electricity. _____
3 Computers is used to control the temperature. _____
4 Cell phones are selled in electronics stores. _____
5 This app can be download onto your smartphone. _____

3 READING: understanding meaning from context

A Read this page from a technology website. Choose a suitable title for the text.

a) Many ways to make phone calls.
b) Smartphones of tomorrow.
c) How to use your phone.

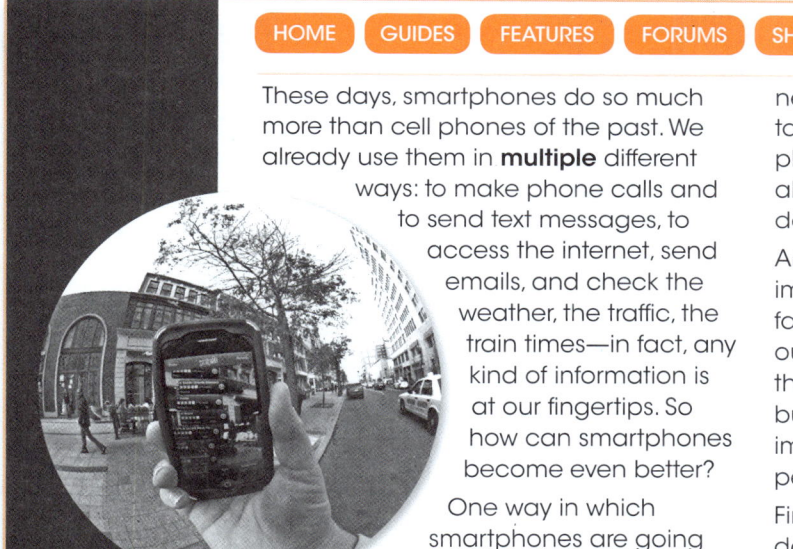

| HOME | GUIDES | FEATURES | FORUMS | SHOP | REVIEWS | NEWS | PODCASTS |

These days, smartphones do so much more than cell phones of the past. We already use them in **multiple** different ways: to make phone calls and to send text messages, to access the internet, send emails, and check the weather, the traffic, the train times—in fact, any kind of information is at our fingertips. So how can smartphones become even better?

One way in which smartphones are going to **improve** is that they will be able to **interact** with the environment. For example, if you visit a new place, you can hold up your phone, take a picture of the place, and your phone will tell you all kinds of information about where you are and what you can do there.

Another **development** will be 3D imaging. We will not only see our friends' faces on the screen, their image will pop out, and you'll see their whole body, and they'll move around just like a real person, but much smaller. This will enhance and improve the way we interact with other people via our phones.

Finally, when you want your phone to do something, you won't need to type anything. You can just speak to the phone, and the phone will **carry out** your instructions.

B Read the text again and look at the words in bold. Look at the context carefully and choose the correct meaning.

1 multiple   a) a few   b) many   c) interesting
2 improve   a) add   b) invent   c) become better
3 interact   a) respond to   b) change   c) speak to
4 development   a) improvement   b) equipment   c) statement
5 carry out   a) do   b) tell   c) create

A Look at the pictures. Complete the sentences about each one using the simple past passive of the verbs in parentheses.

1 The first photograph _____ in 1826. (*take*)

2 The first phone call _____ in 1876. (*make*)

3 The first computer mouse _____ in 1963. (*invent*)

4 The first digital cameras _____ in 1991. (*develop*)

5 The first camera phones _____ in Japan in 2001. (*sell*)

B Write the questions and sentences using the simple past passive. Use *by* if necessary.

1 When / the World Wide Web / create ?

_____

Tim Berners-Lee / 1989

_____

2 When / the first iPhones® / produce ?

_____

2007

_____

3 When / the Apple® logo / design ?

_____

Rob Janoff / 1977

_____

4 When / the computer mouse / invent ?

_____

Douglas Engelbart / 1963

_____

5 VOCABULARY: technology

A Complete the sentences with words in the box.

| add   back up   click   install   log on   print out   right-click   type in |

1 You need to _____ your files regularly if you don't want to lose them.
2 Just _____ on the browser icon and the internet will open up on your desktop.
3 Why don't you _____ this antivirus program on your computer?
4 I want to _____ to my email account, but I can't remember my password.
5 If you _____ your username and password, you can see your account details.
6 You can _____ on the file name and select "send" to save the file on your flash drive.
7 When your transaction is complete, you can _____ this message for your files.
8 Some people _____ all their friends' names to their social-network page.

B Complete the text with words from Exercise A.

MAGIC FILE ORGANIZER:
Save time and money!

Stressed out with documents you can't find? Need help with organizing your files more efficiently? Use our website! It's easy. Just **(1)** _____ with your username and password. Then **(2)** _____ the name of your file in the search box. If you want to **(3)** _____ one of our programs, **(4)** _____ on the icon and select "download." If you want to **(5)** _____ a document, just **(6)** _____ on the printer icon at the top of the page. Worried about losing your files when your computer crashes? Just **(7)** _____ your files on our memory cloud! Tell your friends! Why not **(8)** _____ us to your social-network page?

6 SPEAKING: expressing uncertainty

A 🎧 26 Listen to the conversations. What kind of gadget or device is each person trying to use?

1 _____
2 _____
3 _____
4 _____

B Listen again. Which phrases for expressing uncertainty do you hear? Write the number of the conversation.

☐ I guess so.   ☐ I'm not sure.   ☐ I suppose so.
☐ I think …   ☐ Maybe …   ☐ … probably …

Listen and write

A 🎧 **27** Listen to an interview with Tracy talking about a gadget she can't live without. Choose *T* (true) or *F* (false) or *DS* (doesn't say).

1	She doesn't like going out without her phone.	T / F / DS
2	She uses her smartphone mainly for work.	T / F / DS
3	She uses it to communicate with friends.	T / F / DS
4	She doesn't use it to look up information.	T / F / DS
5	She enjoys playing games on it.	T / F / DS
6	She often listens to music on it.	T / F / DS

B Listen again and write six ways of using a smartphone mentioned by Tracy.

1 to keep _____
2 to get _____
3 to look up _____
4 to check _____
5 to store her _____
6 to listen to _____

Why do you think Tracy likes her smartphone? _____

C Think of a gadget you can't live without. Make notes in the table below.

Name of gadget	What can it be used for?	Why do you like it?

Over to You

D ✏️ Use your notes from Exercise C to write a paragraph in your notebook about your favorite gadget.

DOWN TIME

A Put the pieces together to make six gadgets. Write the letters of the pieces in the table. Then write the names of the gadgets next to the letters.

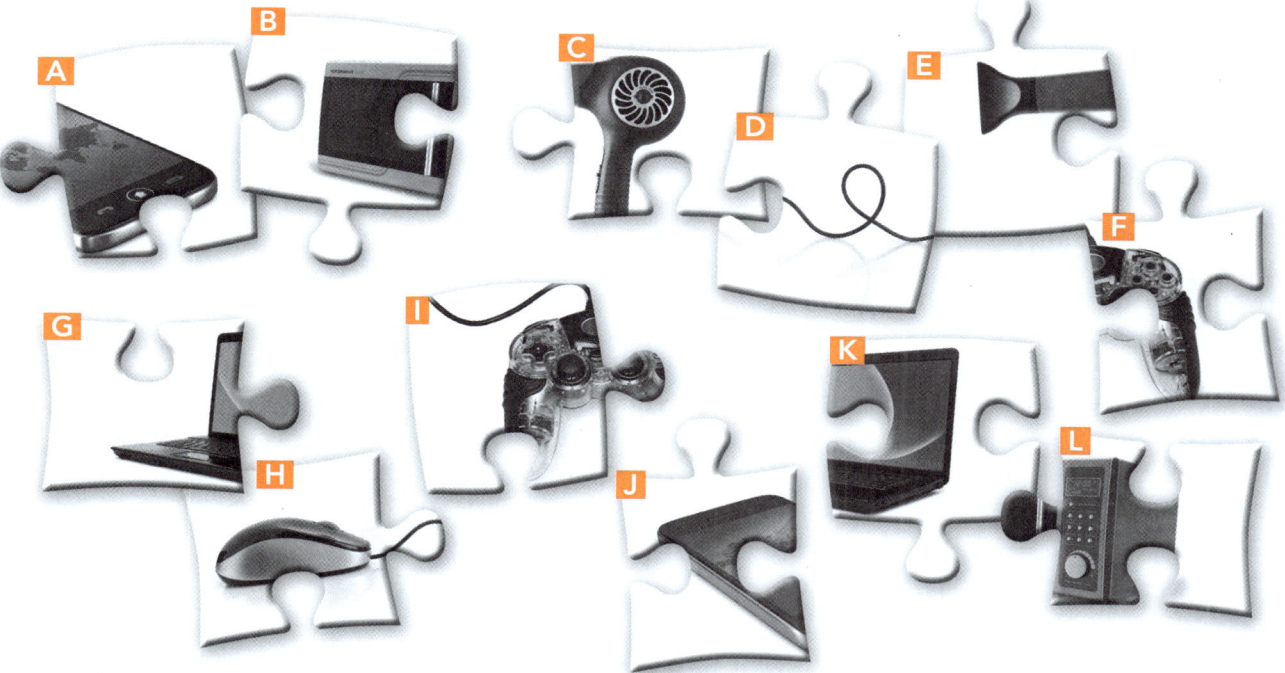

	Puzzle piece	Name of gadget
1		
2		
3		
4		
5		
6		

B Write the name of each type of material. Then unscramble the shaded letters to find the name of a gadget.

Mystery gadget: _ _ _ _ _ _ _

1 VOCABULARY: describing relationships

A Match the phrases to their definitions.

1 admire
2 get along with
3 have arguments
4 make up
5 share the same values
6 go through

a) to experience
b) to agree about the important things in life
c) to disagree
d) to be friends with someone
e) to become friendly again after an argument
f) to respect or look up to someone

B 🎧 **28** **Complete the sentences with words from Exercise A. Then listen and check your answers.**

The person I **(1)** _____ most in my family is my mother. She works really hard to make sure our home is comfortable and clean, and she always makes delicious food for us. We don't really appreciate her enough.

I have two sisters and one brother. We **(2)** _____ from time to time, but we usually **(3)** _____ again soon after. I'd say I **(4)** _____ all of them, especially with my brother. He's my best friend.

I think that the younger generation often has different opinions than their parents.

They don't always **(5)** _____, but I think that's something we all **(6)** _____ as we grow up.

2 GRAMMAR: zero and first conditionals

A Decide if the sentence is in the zero conditional or first conditional.

1 If you don't make mistakes, you won't learn anything.
   a) zero conditional   b) first conditional
2 You'll learn a lot if you listen to your parents.
   a) zero conditional   b) first conditional
3 Our parents get upset if we don't do our homework.
   a) zero conditional   b) first conditional
4 If parents are too strict, their children won't obey them.
   a) zero conditional   b) first conditional
5 If I need advice, I ask my parents first.
   a) zero conditional   b) first conditional
6 If my friend has a problem, I try to help him or her.
   a) zero conditional   b) first conditional

WATCH OUT!

✗ If you will help me, I help you.
✓ _____

B Choose the correct options to complete the sentences.

Zero conditionals

1 If we have / will have a fight, we try / will try to make up soon after.
2 My parents get / will get upset if I don't / won't obey them.
3 If I don't / won't understand a question, I usually ask / will ask my teacher.
4 You find / will find a solution more easily if you talk / will talk about your problems.

First conditionals

5 If you give / will give him a chance, I think you get / will get along well.
6 I try / will try to help you with your homework if you call / will call me later.
7 If he doesn't / won't come home by 10 p.m., he doesn't / won't go out again this month.
8 We won't be / aren't tired tomorrow if we go / will go to sleep early tonight.

C There is one mistake in each sentence. Find and correct it.

1 If I won't have breakfast, I can't concentrate.

_____

2 You will feel tired if you won't get enough sleep.

_____

3 We won't get to school on time if we won't leave now.

_____

4 Our parents get worried if we not home on time.

_____

3 VOCABULARY: values

A Match the sentences to the values they express.

1 Having a permanent job with a good salary is important to me.
2 I hate having to borrow money or ask for help.
3 I love to discover new places and have new experiences.
4 It's important to share my ideas through art, writing, or music.
5 I want to be famous and important.
6 I try to give time to people who need help.

a) express creativity
b) help my community
c) be independent
d) have security
e) find adventure
f) have status

B Complete the blog entries with words in the box.

> hard work   have power   having good friendships   help my community   job satisfaction   job security

What values are most important to you in your life?

My job is the most important thing for me. I don't mean a job that pays a lot of money. **(1)** _____ isn't the main thing, but a job that I believe in and that gives me **(2)** _____ .

In addition to work and family, I think it's important to **(4)** _____ . I work as a volunteer in a hospital, and it makes me feel good to help other people. People really appreciate my help.

I think that **(3)** _____ is the most important thing. I like to spend time with people I love and that takes time and energy.

My goal is to **(5)** _____ and be successful. And **(6)** _____ is the only way to get success. If you're lazy, you won't get anywhere.

4 LISTENING: understanding agreement and disagreement

A 🎧 **29** Listen to the conversation. Do the speakers generally agree or disagree?

B Listen again. Which statements do both speakers agree about and which do they disagree about?

1 People are more willing to change their jobs these days.   agree / disagree
2 People are unhappy if they don't get promoted quickly.   agree / disagree
3 Work isn't important to people these days.   agree / disagree
4 People have a better balance of work and free time these days.   agree / disagree

C Listen again. Number these expressions in the order that you hear them.

☐ Actually, I think you're right.
☐ I'm not sure about that.
☐ Exactly.
☐ Yes, that's true.
☐ Well, I think …
☐ I think you're forgetting that …

5 GRAMMAR: second conditional

A Choose the correct option.

1 If I had / have enough money, I'd buy a bigger house and a new car.
2 Will / Would you change your job if they offered you more money?
3 If I worked at home, I could / can spend more time with my family.
4 I won't / wouldn't be happy if I lived away from home.
5 What would / will you do if you had a year off?
6 If you didn't work so hard, you won't / wouldn't feel so tired.
7 I'm sure you would / will be happier if you had more free time.
8 What would you do if you are / were in my shoes?

B Read each question and choose one option. Then write a sentence to say what you would do. Use the second conditional.

1 You suddenly lose your job.
   a) look for a new job right away
   b) take a year off and travel
   c) decide to do something new
   If _____ .

2 You find $100 in a wallet on the bus.
   a) tell the bus driver
   b) take it to the police
   c) take it home
   If _____ .

3 You see a small child crying in the supermarket.
   a) call the store manager
   b) sit down and talk to the child
   c) not do anything
   If _____ .

4 You have an argument with your brother or sister.
   a) apologize and make up
   b) cry and feel miserable
   c) not say anything
   If _____ .

6 WRITING: paragraphs

A Read the topic sentence for a paragraph. Decide which five sentences are appropriate supporting sentences for the topic. Then number them in the best order.

Topic sentence: Many young people take a year off before they start college.
- [ ] It is an opportunity to get real-life experience.
- [ ] It is difficult to live at home when you're at college.
- [ ] They can think carefully about what they want to study at college.
- [ ] They can travel to other countries, or find a job.
- [ ] It can be a lot of fun.
- [ ] It helps young people develop confidence and maturity.

B Write the paragraph in your notebook. Use these words to introduce the supporting details.
- For example,
- Also,
- In addition,
- Finally,

C 30 Listen to one possible answer.

Read and write

A Read Xiang's essay about personal values and circle T (true) or F (false).

My personal values

    Children learn about values within their family. These values can be very strong and last a lifetime. My parents taught my brother, my sister, and me that it is important to have our own opinions, and to respect other people's opinions, too. For example, whenever I had an argument with my brother or sister, our parents asked us to explain what the argument was about and why we disagreed. This way, we learned to listen to each other. If people listen to each other, they can learn to respect different opinions and values.

    I also learned that it is important to work hard. We had to do jobs around the house, such as washing the dishes, cleaning our rooms, or watering the plants in the garden to earn our allowance. When we were older, we had part-time jobs to earn money to buy things we wanted like comics or CDs. If you have to work for your money, you are more careful about how to spend it.

    I admire my parents because they taught us important values. In the future, if I have children, I'll try to help them develop their identity and to be independent. If I listen to their opinions and show that we can love and respect each other, it will give them a good example to follow in their lives.

1	Xiang's parents taught her to express her opinions.	T / F
2	She sometimes disagreed with her brother and sister.	T / F
3	She never had to do chores for her allowance.	T / F
4	She always had a lot of money as a child.	T / F
5	She spent more money than she had.	T / F
6	She wants her children to be independent.	T / F

Notice how Xiang introduces a personal value. Then she gives an example. Then she describes what she learned.

B Complete the chart with your own ideas.

Personal values	Examples	If you become a parent, how will you share these values with your children?
1 _____	1 _____	1 _____
2 _____	2 _____	2 _____

Over to You

C ✎ Use your notes in Exercise B to write a paragraph in your notebook about your personal values.

WRITING TUTOR

My parents taught me …
I also learned from my parents that …
For example, …
This way …
If …, then you …

DOWN TIME

A Read the clues. Complete the crossword.

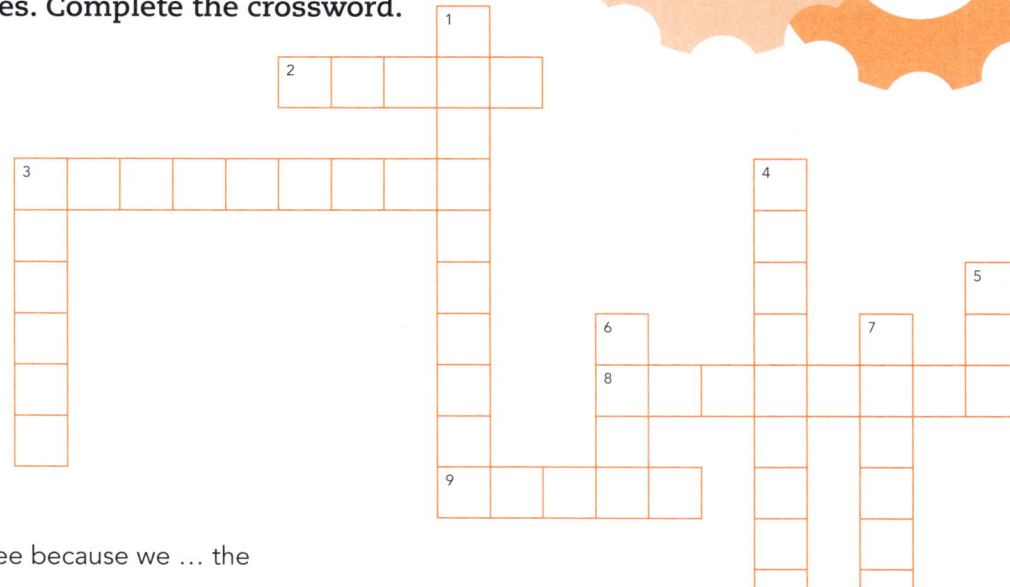

Across
2 We usually agree because we … the same values.

3 … is important to me. I love traveling and having new experiences.

8 I don't like having an … with a friend.

9 Politicians usually have a lot of …

Down
1 I enjoy spending time with my friends. … is important to me.

3 I … my brother because he is very creative.

4 I like to help others in my … so I do a lot of charity work.

5 I try to … along with everyone in my family and we have a good time together.

6 Sometimes we disagree, but we … up soon after.

7 I want a job that's safe and has a lot of …

B Match the parts of the words in the boxes to find seven words for values in our lives. Then write them in order of importance for you.

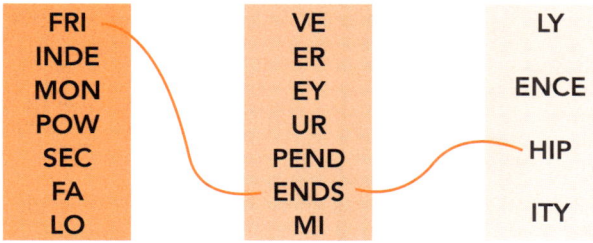

FRI	VE	LY
INDE	ER	
MON	EY	ENCE
POW	UR	
SEC	PEND	HIP
FA	ENDS	
LO	MI	ITY

1 _____   4 _____   7 _____

2 _____   5 _____

3 _____   6 _____

Audio script

UNIT 1

Track 01

A: What do you mainly use your laptop for?

B: Oh, I browse the internet looking for new music and music websites.

A: Do you shop online?

B: Yes, I often download songs that I like and put them on my MP3 player.

A: What about social media? How often do you use sites like Facebook, for example?

B: A lot. I'm in a band and we have a Facebook page. I use it to post pictures or upload videos of our concerts. We also use it to blog about what we're doing as a band.

A: How about Twitter—do you tweet a lot?

B: All the time! It's a great way to get publicity.

A: Great! So it's easy to find you then?

B: Sure! Just google our name—the Martian Rockets!

Track 02

1 A: I remember when I failed my driver's test.
   B: Were you upset about it?
   A: Yes, I was. But I passed the second time.

2 A: Do you remember when we first opened our bookstore?
   B: We were so happy and excited about it.
   A: Yes, we were.

3 A I remember when I started college.
   B: Were you excited about it?
   A: No, I was worried about it. Everything was new and different.

4 A Do you remember when someone stole my bag on the bus?
   B: You were very upset about it.
   A: No, I wasn't. I was angry and a little shocked by it— that's all.

Track 03

I remember when we had our graduation ceremony from high school. It was a very emotional day. Half of my friends were leaving our hometown to go away to college, and I felt upset about it. The ceremony was in the school gym, and I was amazed at how many people were there. I went up on the stage to read my speech. At first, my knees were really shaking, and I couldn't breathe! I started to panic. But then I saw my parents' faces and all my friends. They were smiling and looked so happy. And suddenly I felt very relaxed and confident. I gave the best speech of my life! Two years later, and I'm still in touch with my best friends from high school. We keep in touch by email, and we often chat online. Some of them write blogs about their lives, and we try to meet once a year for our school reunion.

UNIT 2

Track 04

A: What do you think of this exhibition, Nina?

B: It's incredible. Look at this painting. It has so many colors in it!

A: Yes, but what is it? Is it a man with a bicycle on his head? It's weird.

B: But you don't have to understand it — it's art! It makes you think about how to look at things. I think it's fascinating.

A: But look at this picture. It's just a square and a circle. Isn't that a little dull?

B: Not at all! It's amazing!

Track 05

A: How did you like the movie?

B: Oh, it wasn't bad … well, actually, I thought it was pretty dull.

A: Oh, yeah? Don't you like comedies?

B: I do …, but they aren't as good as action movies or thrillers. What did you think?

A: Oh, I liked it. He's one of my favorite movie directors. I really think this comedy was even better than his last one.

UNIT 3

Track 06

1 I'm going on a road trip across the U.S.A. I'm taking my international driver's license, and I'll also need my passport, of course, and a very good map!

2 I'm going on a beach vacation to Hawaii. Lots of swimming and sunbathing, so I'm taking plenty of sunscreen, and of course my sunglasses, too. And just in case I want to do some sightseeing, I'll get a good guidebook.

3 Now, let's see if I have everything. Here's my suitcase, and I can't forget my wallet and my tickets, and there's one more thing … ah yes, my toothbrush!

Track 07

1 A: Can I borrow your newspaper?
   B: Sorry. I'm still reading it.

2 A: May I sit here?
   B: Sure. Go ahead.

3 A: Could you open the window, please?
   B: I'm sorry, I can't. The window is broken.

4 A: Can you help me with my bag, please?
   B: Certainly. No problem.

Track 08

A: Let's get away somewhere different for our vacation this year. Why do we always have to go to the same place? Could we go somewhere different for a change?

B: We don't always go to the same place. Last time we went to Barbados, and the time before it was Jamaica!

A: That's what I mean. We always go to the same kind of place—a beach resort where there's nothing to do except swim and sit on the beach. Can we go somewhere *interesting*?

B: But that's the whole point. You go on vacation to get away from it all … to stop being busy all the time. What's wrong with that?

A: That's *your* ideal vacation, but it's not mine! I like to see interesting sights like ruins and museums, and go to concerts, and learn about different cultures.

B: That sounds much too busy for me … I like to relax, read a book, sit in the sun, go for a swim …

A: Yes … and that's what we always end up doing.

UNIT 4

Track 09

1 A: Have you ever bought a lottery ticket?
   B: Yes, but I never win anything. I think they're a waste of time and money.
   A: Oh, I don't think so. Some of my friends have won …

2 A: Have you ever swum with sharks?
   B: No way! That's too scary!
   A: Yeah, that's true.

3 A: Have you ever been to any music festivals?
   B: No, I haven't. Personally, I think the tickets are too expensive these days.
   A: Yes, I know!

4 A: In my opinion, people use their cell phones way too much.
   B: Oh, I don't know. Cell phones are really useful for staying in touch.
   A: Really?

Track 10

1 **A:** I heard this strange noise in the yard. So I went outside, and suddenly a black cat jumped out at me from behind the tree, and I screamed.

B: Were you scared?

A: Yes! I've never been so scared in my life!

2 **A:** I went to see a play last week.

B: Was it good?

A: Yes, it was amazing. But about halfway through, my cell phone went off.

B: Oh, no!

A: I know, terrible, isn't it? I was so embarrassed.

3 **A:** I started that new computer class last week.

B: How did it go?

A: Well, I thought I knew something about computers when I went in, but when I came out, I felt …

B: … confused?

A: Yes.

UNIT 5

Track 11

1 **A:** Hi. Great music!

B: Yes, this music is great for dancing.

2 **A:** Are you enjoying the concert?

B: It's cool! This band is so good live.

3 **A:** So, have you seen this band before?

B: Yes, I have. I saw them last year. You should buy their album.

4 **A:** Excuse me. Do you know anything about this album?

B: Yes, I downloaded it last week. It's really catchy!

Track 12

1 **A:** I really love reggae. I listen to it all the time.

B: Oh, yeah? I like blues and soul music more. Oh, excuse me—it's late, so I'd better call home.

A: Sure, go ahead.

2 **A:** I saw this cool band last week. They played a fusion of jazz and rock. It was fantastic.

B: Sounds amazing. Hey, I'm sorry, I should go now. It was nice to meet you.

A: Yeah, nice talking to you, too.

3 **A:** Are you enjoying this music? I think it's great.

B: Yes, me too. I love this kind of music. It's so cool.

A: Do you come here often?

4 **A:** Have you listened to this new album?

B: No, is it any good?

A: Yeah, really expressive. What kind of music do you like?

Track 13

Tania: I listen to all kinds of music, but my favorite is African music. I like musicians from Senegal and from Nigeria. One of my favorite singers is Angélique Kidjo. She's from France, but she originally comes from Mali. I love her music because it has wonderful rhythms and is so easy to dance to. Sometimes her songs are very upbeat and happy, and other times they can be so, so sad. It's very expressive.

Nick: I listen to music all the time—on the train, on the computer, everywhere. I like pop music and techno dance music, but I really like electronic music. My favorite singer is Björk. She's from Iceland and she sings in English. She does a lot of really unusual experimental stuff. It's kind of a fusion of electronica and pop-rock. I like her music because she's always trying something new.

Chris: I've always loved soul music and blues. My favorite singer is Adele. She's a British singer, and I think she has a wonderful voice—really powerful. And she composes her own songs, too. They're kind of a mixture of blues, pop, and soul. They're full of emotion and very catchy, too! I love to sing along with her—when I'm alone, of course!

UNIT 6

Track 14

A: As you can see, this room is bright and sunny. There's a gorgeous large window with a view of the park, and plenty of space for a bed and look, a large closet.

B: Oh, look! There are extra closets through here, too.

A: That's right, plenty of storage space! The bathroom is through here—definitely the most up-to-date design …

B: Ooh yes, this is very stylish … look at this shower and bathtub. This looks like marble.

A: Yes, it's real Italian marble. And isn't this living room beautiful? You have your armchairs and sofa over there … TV and coffee table over here …

B: Perfect for entertaining.

A: Absolutely … and walk right through here … This is the kitchen. Just look at these countertops, and the new stove, refrigerator over here. And beautiful cabinets.

B: Yes, and there's even space for a dining table. Hmmm, now what did you say about the price?

Track 15

A: Today's *Advice Corner* comes from Maureen Abbott. And she's going to tell us about how to make more space in our closets!

B: It's really easy to make more storage space in your cabinets and closets if you go about it systematically. The first thing you need to do is to empty your closets and sort everything into three bags: things you need every week or every day, things that you only need sometimes, and things you can throw away. Take this opportunity to get rid of things you'll never wear or use again. The rule is: if you haven't worn it for a year, throw it away.
Next, separate your clothes into summer and winter clothing. In the summer, you can store your winter clothing in boxes under the bed to make more space in your closets.
After that, put all the things you need every day on the middle shelf of your closet. Put all the things you don't need very often on the top shelf, or right at the bottom. Then, you need to organize the shelves so that you can find things quickly when you need them. Use small baskets and boxes to help you organize small objects like jewelry or makeup or CDs. This can save you time when you are looking for something in a hurry.
Finally, think about using the vertical space in your closets. It's useful to have a lot of hooks in your closets to hang up objects like your umbrella or hairdryer or hats and scarves.

A: Thanks so much, Maureen, for these wonderful ideas and tips. I'm going to get started on my closets tomorrow!

UNIT 7

Track 16

A: Welcome to our "Guess the Food" contest! Four volunteers from the audience are going to wear a blindfold and taste these foods without seeing or smelling them. Can they guess what they're eating? We start with volunteer number one.

B: Mmm … I'm eating this with a spoon. It's a little greasy, but it's also crunchy, salty, and sweet at the same time. Oh, it tastes like nuts. I think I know exactly what it is. It's … peanut butter!

A: Good job! That's the correct answer! Now volunteer number two.

C: This is interesting, OK, I'm eating this with a fork. It's creamy and sweet. Definitely sweet with a sort of lemony flavor, oh, and it has a crunchy cookie-type of base at the bottom—mmm, delicious! I think it's … cheesecake.

A: Yes, that's right! It was lemon cheesecake. Congratulations! And now volunteer number three.

D: Let's see, I'm holding a piece of this food in my fingers. It's … it's very juicy … ahhh, it's really sour! That's … a lemon.

A: Sorry! Are you OK? But you did a good job. And you were right. This is a lemon! And now our last volunteer, number four.

E: It's soft. I'm eating this with a fork, but it's very salty … oh, yes, and very, very hot and spicy … oh, it's burning my mouth! I recognize this. It's fried beans with chili peppers.

A: Spicy! That's right! Good job and thank you to all of our volunteers today!

Track 17

A: Thanks so much for helping me with the picnic today, Yuki.

B: No problem! I'm happy to help. I hope I got enough food at the supermarket.

A: OK, let's check the list and see. How many bags of potato chips did you get?

B: Ten, and six packages of cookies, too.

A: That's great. And how many cans of soda?

B: Twelve—one for each of us. And two large bottles of water.

A: Perfect! And I already have a large bottle of orange juice. Did you get any bread?

B: Yes, I bought two loaves of bread, three jars of peanut butter, and three jars of jam.

A: Wonderful! I think that will be enough for everyone!

B: There's only one problem. I'm on a diet, and I can't eat any of this food. So I brought some apples for *my* lunch!

Track 18

1 While I was in Australia, I visited a restaurant that served crocodile stew. The crocodile meat was extremely tough and not that tasty. In fact, it was too difficult to chew, and I gave up halfway through.

2 In Sweden they eat this strange kind of pickled herring. It's kept in a wooden barrel for a year. You eat it with potatoes, a little onion, and a few tomatoes. It's usually served on thin, hard bread. It tastes delicious, kind of sour and sweet at the same time—but the smell is disgusting!

3 The most unusual food I have ever tasted is a peanut butter and jam sandwich. I can't believe people eat that for lunch in the U.S.A. Why would you put salty food and sweet food together like that? It's not healthy enough, and it tastes really strange.

UNIT 8

Track 19

A: Have Mike and Rachel broken up? I haven't seen them together recently.

B: Yes, Mike's going out with Julianna now. I think they just got engaged.

A: Really? They haven't known each other that long, right?

B: No, they met on a blind date about a month ago. The next day, he asked her out again, and the rest is history.

A: That's great news! I hope they'll be happy!

Track 20

The Eastern Brown Pelican is a brownish-gray bird with a large pouch under its beak. Pelicans live in Florida in very large numbers in the bird preservation area known as Pelican Island.

Pelicans reproduce once a year, laying two to three eggs at a time. The male and female pelicans work together to make the nest and incubate the eggs. The males collect the building material and the females build the nest. The nests are on the ground. They incubate the eggs for 28 to 30 days.

It is amazing that Pelican chicks can learn to communicate with their parents while they are still inside the egg. Pelican chicks make sounds from inside the egg when they are too hot or cold!

Both parents feed and care for their young. They take turns catching fish during the day, and bring the fish back to the nest, carrying it in their beaks. The young pelicans dip their beaks into the parents' beaks to get the fish. Baby pelicans often learn to swim before they learn to fly.

UNIT 9

Track 21

1 **A:** Hi, Dale. How's the weather in Boston today? Is it cold?

   B: Yes, it's very, very cold! We've had about two feet of snow since yesterday, and we spent all this morning shoveling the sidewalk and trying to dig our car out! The kids love it—they made an amazing snowman!

2 **A:** Oh, hi, Jackie. Where are you?

   B: We're on the beach! It's a gorgeous sunny day here in Miami—not a cloud in the sky, and the temperature is wonderful! It's hot, but not too hot— around 80 degrees.

   A: Sounds perfect, I wish I was there!

3 **A:** How's the weather in San Francisco today?

   B: Oh, you know … the usual … it's a cold gray day, very cloudy. I think it's going to rain soon. I wanted to go out for a walk at lunchtime, but it was too wet and too windy.

4 **A:** What's the weather like there today?

   B: Oh, it's kind of nasty, you know. It was very cold overnight, about 30 degrees, and now it's foggy, and visibility is really low. The weather forecast says it's going to get stormy later this afternoon. Not great, really.

Track 22

1 **A:** Could you make copies of these letters, please?

   B: I might not have time before lunch. Is that OK?

   C: Sorry to interrupt. Could I borrow your pen for a moment?

   B: Yes, of course. Here you are.

2 **A:** Do you want to have lunch in the cafeteria?

   B: Yes, I'd like that very much!

   C: Sorry, can I interrupt for a second? Which way is the cafeteria?

   B: Oh, we're going that way. Why don't you come with us?

3 **A:** Could I get some information about the new courses, please?

   B: Yes, sure. Here's the latest course listing and class timetable. Do you think you might be interested?

   C: Excuse me, can I ask a quick question? Could I have one of those timetables, please?

   B: Yes, of course. Here you go.

Track 23

1 **A:** What are you going to do to help the environment?

   B: I'm not going to drive my car when I can use public transportation. What about you?

   A: We're going to save electricity by using solar panels on our house.

   B: That's a good idea! Will there be enough sunshine?

   A: Well, there won't be as much sunshine in the winter, but there should be enough daylight.

2 **A:** I'm going to join this new climate change organization.

   B: Really? What are they going to do to stop climate change?

   A: They're going to make simple changes. For example, I'm going to ride my bike to work, and I'm not going to use plastic bags.

   B: That's a good idea! Maybe I'll do that, too!

Track 24

1   I'm going to live on a small island in Greece. I'll live in a small village near the sea. The weather there is warm and sunny every day. The beach has beautiful white sand. The sea is clear and blue, and the water is warm. I'll have a small house on the beach and a little fishing boat. Every morning, I'll go out and catch fish. In the afternoon, I'll take a nap under a palm tree. My lifestyle will be very relaxed.

2   I'm going to live in a small village in Tuscany in Italy. There are hills and fruit trees all around the area. The summers are hot and the winters are warm, but never cold. I'll live on a farm and grow olive trees. I'll also have a large vegetable garden and a lot of flowers. Some people might say it's a little lonely, but I love peace and quiet, and all my friends will visit me, so it'll be wonderful!

3   I'm going to live in New York City. I'll have a small apartment in Manhattan, not far from all the stores and restaurants. I know it's noisy, and expensive, too. But I won't need a car because public transportation is so good, and there are plenty of good places to eat that aren't at all expensive. I'll go out to the theater and to art exhibitions, and enjoy eating out every day.

UNIT 10

Track 25

1   A: I don't like giving parties at home. It's too much work!
    B: I completely agree! I'd much rather go out to a restaurant or a dance club.

2   A: Do you know that new Italian restaurant on the corner? We went there last week, and it was really expensive.
    B: I'm not sure I agree with you. We went there on Tuesday night, and they had a special offer—two meals for the price of one!

3   A: Have you been to that new music club? It's called Maxine's. We went there on Saturday.
    B: Yes, I have. What did you think of it?
    A: I didn't like it all. It was too loud and very crowded.
    B: You're absolutely right. There's too much noise, and the atmosphere is awful.

UNIT 11

Track 26

1   A: Do you know how to use this printer?
    B: Um … I'm not sure … I think if you press this button here … oops, no, that's not it …
    A: Oh, well, don't worry …

2   A: Can you help me with this laptop?
    B: Sure, what do you need?
    A: I'm just trying to turn it on.
    B: Hmm … let's see … you probably need to press this button here.

3   A: How does this smartphone work? I want to access my messages. Is it this button here?
    B: Um … I guess so … oh, it looks a little different from mine …
    A: I've tried this button, but nothing happened.
    B: Oh. I see. Maybe you could try this one …

4   A: Can you show me how to use this coffee maker? Do I press this button first?
    B: Oh, I suppose so … let's take a look. First, you select the type of coffee …
    A: And then the start button?
    B: Yes, that's it!

Track 27

A: What's one gadget you can't live without?
B: Oh, that definitely has to be my smartphone! I can't go anywhere without it!
A: What do you generally use it for?
B: Oh, everything! Well, I suppose mainly to make phone calls and send emails and text messages.
A: So … to keep in touch with your friends?
B: That's right. But I also use it as a calendar, and to check where I'm going, and what I'm supposed to be doing!
A: I see, and what else do you use it for?
B: Well, I use it to get directions if I'm going somewhere new, or I use it to look up times of shows or movies, or check reviews of restaurants … and then I have all my pictures stored on there. So I can send pictures to people or show them my pictures.
A: It saves having to carry stuff around with you.
B: Absolutely! It's small enough to go in my pocket. And then, of course, I listen to music on it. I just snap these headphones in, and that's it—I'm in another world!

UNIT 12

Track 28

The person I admire most in my family is my mother. She works really hard to make sure our home is comfortable and clean, and she always makes delicious food for us. We don't really appreciate her enough.

I have two sisters and one brother. We have arguments from time to time, but we usually make up again soon after. I'd say I get along with all of them, especially with my brother. He's my best friend.

I think that the younger generation often has different opinions than their parents. They don't always share the same values, but I think that's something we all go through as we grow up.

Track 29

A: Do you think people's attitudes and expectations about work are changing these days?
B: Well, I think people are more willing to change their jobs and move to another company, or another city, to find better work. Definitely.
A: Yes, that's true. And I also think that when people start a new job, they expect to learn skills they can transfer to another job later. I see that a lot when graduates apply for their first job. They always ask about training and promotions.
B: Yes, but … I think that then they get dissatisfied if they aren't promoted quickly enough.
A: I'm not sure about that. I think people understand that a promotion is the result of hard work *and* experience. And this takes some time.
B: But that's exactly the problem! People's attitudes about hard work are different these days. I think they're less interested in working hard.
A: Hmm. I think you're forgetting that lifestyles have changed. I'd say people have more outside interests, and they're probably better at keeping a work-life balance. But this doesn't mean that they don't work hard.
B: Actually, I think you're right. In my company, there's a sports and fitness club, and they even have yoga classes People aren't stuck to their desks all day.
B: Exactly. And then they don't get so stressed about work … that's a very good thing!

Track 30

Many young people take a year off before they start college. It is an opportunity to get real-life experience. For example, they can travel to other countries, or find a job. Also, they can think carefully about what they want to study at college. In addition, it helps young people develop confidence and maturity. Finally, it can be a lot of fun.

Answer key

UNIT 1

Section 1
Exercise A
1 browse 2 online 3 download 4 post
5 upload 6 blog 7 tweet 8 google

Exercise B
1 shop 2 blog 3 upload
4 download 5 upload 6 browse

Section 2
Exercise A
1 going 2 playing 3 swimming
4 writing 5 dancing

Exercise B
1 was chatting
2 wasn't sending
3 wasn't chatting
4 was shopping
5 Was, shopping, Yes, was

6 Was, downloading, No, wasn't
7 Were, sending, No, weren't
8 Were, studying, Yes, were

Watch out!
He wasn't doing his homework this morning.

Exercise D
Ben: was celebrating
Sam: were listening
Louise: wasn't sleeping
Gina: was watching, was playing
Vicky: was sending

Section 3
Exercise A
1 angry 2 amazed 3 surprised 4 excited 5 happy
6 upset 7 interested 8 worried

Exercise B
1 upset 2 excited and happy 3 worried 4 upset

Section 4
Exercise A
1 We, It 2 it, They 3 She, them 4 She, it
Exercise B
1 b 2 a 3 a 4 b

Section 5
Exercise A
1 was living, wrote
2 got, were traveling
3 was studying, stole
4 were cleaning, found
5 met, was studying
6 was researching, found

Exercise B
1 I was chatting online when I heard the crash.
2 We didn't go out while it was raining.
3 Julianne and Kate were having dinner when they heard the news.
4 Were you living in South Korea when you started Korean lessons?

Watch out!
What were you doing when I called you?

Section 6
Exercise A
1 Cool. Did you like it?
2 Yeah? Where?
3 Really? Why? What were you doing?
4 And what about you?
Oh, yeah? How come?

Listen and write
1 his high school graduation
2 upset; half his friends were leaving his hometown to go away to college
3 nervous; there were a lot of people at the ceremony and he had to read a speech on stage
4 relaxed and confident; he saw his parents and friends, and they were smiling and looked happy
5 he gave the best speech in his life

DOWN TIME
Exercise A
Across
4 happy 5 interested 7 surprised 8 amazed
Down
1 angry 2 worried 3 upset 6 excited

Exercise B
1 same, game 2 ride, hide, 3 fine, nine 4 mice, nice

UNIT 2

Section 1
Exercise A
Positive: amazing, awesome, fascinating, hilarious, incredible, interesting
Negative: dull, dumb, ridiculous, terrible, weird

Exercise B
1 a 2 b 3 b 4 a 5 a 6 b

Section 2
Exercise A
1 Museums aren't as interesting as art galleries.
2 Painting isn't as easy as photography.
3 TV shows aren't as good as movies.
4 Country music isn't as dull as hip-hop.

B
1 Horror movies are not as interesting as action movies.
2 Opera is not as exciting as rock music.
3 Classical music concerts are as expensive as operas.
4 Modern art is not as well-liked as classical art.
5 Photography is as difficult as painting.
6 Online games are not as popular as video games.

Watch out!
CDs are as expensive as DVDs.

Section 3
Exercise A
amazing, weird, dull, fascinating, incredible

Exercise B
1 F 2 F 3 T 4 T 5 F

Section 4
Exercise A
1 a music society 2 a language class 3 a comedy show
4 architecture 5 an exhibition

Exercise B
1 go 2 join 3 learn, see, take

Section 5
Exercise A
good, the best
bad, the worst
funny, the funniest
fat, the fattest
beautiful, the most beautiful
strange, the strangest
popular, the most popular
happy, the happiest
interesting, the most interesting
important, the most important

Exercise B

1 least popular 2 most exciting 3 least boring
4 least exciting 5 least interesting 6 most difficult
7 most popular 8 best

Watch out!

Photography is the easiest kind of art to make.

Section 6

Exercise A

1 c 2 a 3 d 4 b

Exercise B

1 Because 2 so 3 Because 4 so

Read and write

A

1 *Prometheus*
2 Sci-fi horror
3 It isn't as scary as the previous movies.
4 Yes. He likes it because of the special effects and computer graphics.

DOWN TIME

Exercise A

1 a 2 b 3 b 4 a 5 a 6 b 7 a 8 a 9 a 10 b

Exercise B

```
Y T F G R E B I H T C O P H V
J N I E P A D U T N L S E O K
A B A L L E T X H L A T R R D
O R L I U E J A E O S Z U R J
Z A T E R U P W U S K I O E F
R S S E F Z I S X F I T T R F
D D Y R X H B A C D C A E M K
E L O A I H N I M S A O A O O
G W P T H R I J N Z L N S V O
F T H U V O X B V T M C S I W
A T G R O R E A I L U R E E D
B I P E M C L L Q T S F T S P
I J E T X C M E U F I H K Y H
X N A R S D Y T N P C O L F N
R D M U J B N T V C I U N W H
```

1 ballet 2 classical music 3 literature
4 horror movies 5 art exhibition

UNIT 3

Section 1

Exercise A

1 driver's license, passport, map
2 sunscreen, sunglasses, guidebook
3 suitcase, wallet, tickets, toothbrush

Exercise B

1 toothbrush 2 passport 3 driver's license 4 ticket
5 guidebook 6 wallet 7 suitcase 8 map

Exercise C

Suggested answers

1 a passport, a map, a toothbrush, a ticket
3 a ticket, a wallet, a map
4 a guidebook, a passport, a map, a toothbrush, a ticket

Section 2

Exercise A

1 herself 2 themselves 3 yourself
4 ourselves 5 myself 6 himself

Exercise B

1 Alone
2 Without help from another person
3 Subject and object are the same
4 Without help from another person
5 Subject and object are the same
6 Alone

Exercise C

1 yourselves 2 ourselves 3 herself
4 myself 5 yourself

Exercise D

1 He doesn't like traveling <u>by himself</u>.
2 I'd like to pay for <u>myself</u>, please.
3 We can choose the places to visit <u>ourselves</u>.
4 They didn't tell us much about <u>themselves</u>.
5 Please get <u>yourself</u> / <u>yourselves</u> something to eat.
6 Can he carry these bags by <u>himself</u>?

Section 3

Exercise A

1 change 2 find 3 make 4 pack 5 rent 6 check in

Exercise B

1 go 2 find 3 make 4 rent
5 change 6 pack 7 take 8 check in

Section 4

1 They: the tree houses; them: birds and animals;
He: the guide
2 They: ice chairs; them: ice chairs; it: the hotel

Section 5

Exercise A

1 R 2 O 3 P 4 O 5 R

Watch out!

<u>Can/Could</u> you tell me the time, please?

Exercise B

1 Could I have two tickets, please? b in the subway station
2 May I use my cell phone here? d at a hospital
3 Could I get 200 g of olives, please? a in a supermarket
4 Can you carry my suitcase for me? e at a hotel
5 Could I pay by credit card? c in a bookstore

Section 6

Exercise A

N Sorry.   P Go ahead.
P Sure.   P Certainly.
P No problem.   N I'd rather you didn't.
N I'm sorry, I can't   P Of course.

Exercise B

1 Sorry. 2 Go ahead. 3 I'm sorry, I can't. 4 Certainly.

Listen and write

Exercise A

1 T 2 F 3 T 4 F 5 T 6 F

Exercise B

Possible answers

1 To get away from it all; To stop being busy all the time
2 To see interesting sights; To go to concerts; To learn about different cultures

DOWN TIME

Exercise A

1 tickets, map, sunglasses
2 wallet, toothbrush, passport
3 guidebook, driver's license, sunscreen

Exercise B

1 In Picture B, a man is checking in and showing his tickets (not his passport).
2 In Picture B, a woman is waiting in line behind him and holding a guidebook (not a map).
3 In Picture B, a woman is not wearing sunglasses.
4 In Picture B, the man standing next to the woman is holding a briefcase (not a suitcase).
5 In Picture B, the man at the back is wearing shorts (not pants).
6 In Picture B, there is no sunscreen in the suitcase

UNIT 4

Section 1

Exercise A

1 won   2 had   3 lost   4 missed
5 got   6 failed   7 saw   8 found

Watch out!

I missed the last bus home.

Exercise B

1 fail e   2 find f   3 win d   4 miss c   5 have b   6 lose a

Section 2

Exercise A

be, been   eat, eaten   watch, watched
go, gone   give, given   see, seen
work, worked   win, won
find, found   read, read

Exercise B

1 I have never eaten sushi.
2 We have never visited Thailand.
3 I have never won the lottery.
4 She has never seen *Star Trek*.
5 I have never worked in an office.
6 He has never read a newspaper.

Exercise C

1 Have you ever missed a plane?
2 Have you ever lost your passport?
3 Have you ever won a competition?
4 Have you ever written a letter?
5 Have you ever had an accident?
6 Have you ever caught a fish?

Watch out!

I have never seen a giraffe.

Section 3

Exercise A

1 disagree   2 agree   3 agree   4 disagree

Exercise B

1 I don't think so.   3 I know.   4 I don't know.   1 I think …
4 In my opinion, …   3 Personally, I …   2 That's true.

Section 4

Exercise A

1 d   2 f   3 h   4 c   5 g   6 b   7 e   8 a

Exercise B

1 A black cat jumped out at him: afraid
2 His cell phone went off in the middle of a play: embarrassed
3 She started a new computer class: confused

Section 5

Exercise A

for: an hour, six months, three days, two years
since: 2008, last year, November, Wednesday

Exercise B

1 I haven't been to a concert for three months
2 been to Brazil for ten years
3 studied Chinese for four years
4 been in their new home since 2013
5 had this MP3 player since August
6 had our cat for two years

Watch out!

I've lived in this town for three years.

Exercise C

1 have, owned, For   4 haven't seen, for
2 hasn't had, since   5 has, played, Since
3 haven't eaten, since   6 has taught, for

Section 6

Exercise A

1 but   2 and   3 because   4 or   5 so

Read and write

Exercise A

1 b   2 a

DOWN TIME

Exercise A

Across

2 lost   4 eaten   8 ridden   9 seen   10 won

Down

1 flown   3 played   5 drunk   6 been   7 missed

Exercise B

1 proud   2 confused   3 disappointed   4 embarrassed
5 thrilled   6 scared   7 exhausted
Mystery word: excited

UNIT 5

Section 1

Exercise A

1 classical   2 reggae   3 heavy metal   4 country
5 hip-hop   6 Latin   7 jazz   8 dance

Exercise B

1 jazz   2 Latin   3 hip-hip

Section 2

Exercise A

1 SP   2 PP   3 SP   4 PP

Exercise B

1 played   2 have   3 played   4 Did, enjoy   5 did
6 won   7 have, been   8 have   9 went   10 was

Watch out!

I have never written a song.

Exercise C

1 went   2 Have, seen   3 've seen
4 has, played   5 were   6 took
7 bought   8 listened   9 did, do

Section 3

Exercise A

1 a   2 c

Exercise B

1 T   2 F   3 T   4 T   5 F   6 F

Section 4
Exercise A
1 d **2** e **3** f **4** a **5** b **6** c

Exercise B
1 catchy **2** loud **3** repetitive
4 upbeat **5** relaxing **6** old-fashioned

Section 5
Exercise A
1 should **2** should **3** Should
4 shouldn't **5** ought **6** should I

Exercise B
1 e, should **2** d, shouldn't **3** a, should
4 c, ought **5** f, ought **6** b, should

Exercise C
1 Should, shouldn't **2** should, ought **3** Should, should

Section 6
Exercise A
1 b **2** c **3** d **4** a

Exercise B
1 b **2** b **3** a **4** a

Listen and write
Exercise A
Tania: African, Angélique Kidjo, France and Mali, songs are sometimes upbeat and happy, sometimes sad
Nick: electronic, Björk, Iceland, always trying something new
Chris: soul music and blues, Adele, Britain, emotional and catchy

DOWN TIME
Exercise A
1 opera **2** New York **3** New Orleans **4** The Beatles
5 1970s **6** jazz **7** GRAMMY **8** Bob Marley
9 Destiny's Child **10** Adele

Exercise B

```
C O N C E R T W V C
Z A H N D G U L G O
J A Z B V V J S O U
C L A S S I C A L N
S F R R G K E D I T
D U J E C O L P Z R
J S R O P D S J S Y
A I R Q E E B P P F
Z O K S W V P H E H
Z N N M U B L A Z L
```

UNIT 6

Section 1
Exercise A
Possible answers
1 sink, cabinets, refrigerator, dining table
2 sink, toilet, bathtub
3 armchair, sofa, rug, coffee table
4 bed, nightstand, lamp

Exercise B
bathtub, bed, cabinets, coffee table, sofa, shower, stove, TV
Others: armchair, closet, dining table, refrigerator

Section 2
Exercise A
1 have to **2** have to **3** don't need to
4 don't have to **5** don't need to

Exercise B
1 have to **2** don't need to **3** have to

Exercise C
1 have to **2** have to / need to **3** have to / need to
4 doesn't have to **5** have to **6** needs to

Watch out!
We must <u>call</u> the energy company.

Section 3
Exercise A
7

Exercise B
1 Empty your closets.
2 Sort clothes into three bags.
3 Throw away old clothes.
4 Store winter clothing in summer.
5 Organize your shelves.
6 Use boxes to organize small objects.
7 Hang things up on hooks.

Section 4
Exercise A
slow, slowly, more slowly, the most slowly
careful, carefully, more carefully, the most carefully
fast, fast, faster, the fastest
good, well, better, the best
bad, badly, worse, the worst

Exercise B
1 messy **2** stressful **3** efficiently **4** carefully
5 faster **6** more **7** best

Section 5
Exercise A
1 out **2** up **3** away **4** up **5** away **6** up **7** away

Exercise B
1 cleans **2** take **3** put **4** throws **5** picks **6** hangs

Section 6
Exercise A
A When they start college, students often have to choose between living in a dorm or living in a rented house.
B There are many advantages to living in a dorm.
C However, some students prefer to live off-campus in their second or third year.

Read and write
Exercise A
A What's your home like?
B What are some problems?
C Why do you like your home?

DOWN TIME
Exercise A
sofa lamp sink table bed
Secret message: smile

Exercise B
1 The bedroom has a bed and a closet but no nightstand. In picture A, the bedroom has a nightstand.
2 The bathroom has a shower, a bathtub, and a toilet. In picture A, the bathroom has no bathtub.
3 The kitchen has a stove, a refrigerator, and a dining table. In picture A, the kitchen has no dining table.
4 The living room has a sofa and two armchairs, but no rug. In picture A, the living room has a rug.

5 The living room has a coffee table. In picture A, the living room has no coffee table.
6 The living room has a lamp in the corner. In picture A, the lamp is next to the armchair.
7 A woman is taking trash out of the kitchen door. In picture A, a woman is hanging up a coat by the kitchen door.
8 A teenage boy is cleaning up the dishes from the kitchen table after a meal. In picture A, a teenage girl is picking up magazines from the floor in the living room.

UNIT 7

Section 1
Exercise A
1 sweet   **2** salty   **3** sour   **4** crunchy
Exercise B
Suggested answers
1 apple: juicy, crunchy, sweet
2 mango: juicy, sweet
3 cheese: salty, creamy
4 mustard: creamy, spicy
5 ginger: crunchy, spicy
6 potato chips: crunchy, salty, spicy
7 grapefruit: sour, juicy
8 ice cream: sweet, creamy
Exercise C
Volunteer 1
Description: greasy, crunchy, salty, sweet
Mystery food: peanut butter
Volunteer 2
Description: creamy, sweet, crunchy
Mystery food: lemon cheesecake
Volunteer 3
Description: juicy, sour
Mystery food: lemon
Volunteer 4
Description: soft, salty, spicy
Mystery food: fried beans with chili peppers

Section 2
Exercise A
1 The dessert is not creamy enough.
2 The sauce is too spicy.
3 The toast is not crunchy enough.
4 The ice cream is too sweet.

Watch out!
This coffee isn't <u>hot enough</u>.

Exercise B
1 This soup is too cold.
2 This sauce is salty enough.
3 These French fries are too greasy.
4 These grapes aren't sweet enough.
5 This orange isn't juicy enough.
6 These vegetables aren't crunchy enough.
7 This lemonade is sweet enough.

Section 3
Exercise A
1 a box of chocolates
2 a bag of potato chips
3 a can of soup
4 a package of rice
5 a jar of mayonnaise
6 a bottle of water
Exercise B
1 c   **2** c   **3** a   **4** c   **5** a   **6** b
Exercise C
10 bags of potato chips
6 packages of cookies
12 cans of soda
2 bottles of water
2 loaves of bread
3 jars of peanut butter
3 jars of jam

Section 4
Exercise A
1 enough   **2** too many   **3** too much
4 too much   **5** enough   **6** too many
Exercise B
1 less, less   **2** fewer, less   **3** less   **4** fewer   **5** less
Exercise C
1 much   **2** little   **3** few   **4** more   **5** many   **6** lot

Watch out!
I don't drink <u>much</u> tea.

Section 5
1 B   **2** A   **3** D   **4** C

Section 6
Exercise A
a popular American social event
Exercise B
1 a   **2** a
Exercise C
1 a competition   **2** visitors   **3** no   **4** sugar

Listen and write
Exercise A
Speaker 1: C
Speaker 2: B
Speaker 3: A
Exercise B
1 Australia, tough and not that tasty, no
2 Sweden, sweet and sour, yes
3 the U.S.A., salty and sweet, no

DOWN TIME
Exercise A
1 shrimp   **2** pasta   **3** turkey   **4** steak
Exercise B
1 a   **2** a   **3** c   **4** a   **5** c   **6** c   **7** b   **8** c   **9** a   **10** b

UNIT 8

Section 1
Exercise A
1 B   **2** C   **3** E   **4** A   **5** D
Exercise B
1 broken up   **2** going out   **3** got engaged
4 blind date   **5** asked, out

Section 2
Exercise A
1 to see   **2** eat   **3** cooking   **4** to go out
5 to go   **6** have   **7** to cook   **8** watching
Exercise B
1 I would like to go to a party.
2 Would you like to go out for dinner?
3 We would rather not go out tonight.
4 Would you prefer to eat at home?
5 I would prefer not to eat Italian food.
6 Would you rather go to a movie?

Watch out!
I'd rather not <u>see</u> a movie tonight.

Exercise C
1 Would you prefer to go to a movie?
2 Would you prefer to talk in a café?
3 Would you rather meet with a group of friends?
4 Would you rather go dancing?
5 Would you prefer to talk about music?
6 Would you like to have dinner with your parents?

Section 3
Exercise A
1 having—After a preposition
2 Going—Subject
3 dancing, listening—Object
4 talking—After a preposition
5 giving—Object
6 playing—Subject

Exercise B
1 Filling 2 Giving 3 going 4 asking 5 Getting
6 going 7 Chatting 8 dating 9 Meeting 10 making

Watch out!
I really enjoy <u>going</u> to parties.

Exercise C
1 Meeting people at parties is easy.
2 Having dinner with friends is fun.
3 I don't like arguing with friends.
4 I hate being late for a meeting.
5 I'm afraid of going out alone at night.
6 He's nervous about getting engaged.

Section 4
Paragraph 1
a) Males usually fly there from Mexico or Central America before the females.
d) As soon as they arrive, they begin to look for a mating place.
b) It's important for the male to establish his territory around their mating place and guard it against intruders.
Paragraph 2
f) The most important method of attracting the females is to fly around energetically.
e) The males fly high up into the air, and then dive straight down back toward the ground again.
c) Other strategies include singing and flapping their wings as fast as possible to create a loud humming sound.

Section 5
Exercise A
1 T 2 F 3 T 4 F 5 T 6 F

Section 6
Exercise A
1 c 2 f 3 a 4 b 5 d 6 e

Exercise B
1 Did you get hungry?
2 Did you get tired?
3 Did he get angry?
4 Did you get sick?
5 Did he get better?
6 Did you get thirsty?

Read and write
Exercise A

	What did they do on their first date?	How did they feel?	What would they prefer to do on a first date?
Gloria	went to a Chinese restaurant and ate noodles with chopsticks	shy, nervous	eat Mexican food or pizza
Takeo	went bowling	bored	go to a concert

DOWN TIME
Exercise A
1 Tim asked Sue out.
2 Sue and Tim got engaged.
3 Sue and Tim broke up.
4 Sue and Mike went on a date.
5 Sue and Tim got back together again.
6 Sue and Tim got married.

Exercise B
1 hungry 2 thirsty 3 angry 3 bored
5 better 6 scared 7 married
Mystery word: romance

UNIT 9

Section 1
Exercise A
1 snows 2 windy 3 sunny 4 stormy 5 foggy 6 rains

Exercise B
1 cold, snow 2 sunny, cloud, hot
3 cold, cloudy, rain, wet, windy 4 cold, foggy, stormy

Exercise C
1 snow 2 raining 3 stormy 4 wind 5 rain 6 cloudy

Section 2
Exercise A
1 will 2 may 3 will 4 might 5 will 6 might

Exercise B
1 We might go swimming this weekend.
2 I'm sure it won't rain today.
3 We may get a lot of snow this winter.
4 I will definitely go to the beach next weekend.
5 They might not go on vacation this year.
6 It will probably be sunny tomorrow.

Exercise C
Possible answers:
1 a) He may/might not find a new job.
   b) He will get some good advice.
2 a) They will go into the store.
   b) They might/may buy a new dress.
3 a) She will not/won't finish her work today.
   b) She may/might be very tired when she goes home.

Watch out!
We might not <u>have</u> time for coffee.

Section 3
Exercise A
1 Excuse me, can I interrupt you for a second?
2 Excuse me, can I ask a quick question?
3 Sorry to interrupt, but what was the homework?

Exercise B

	Topic of main conversation	Reason for interrupting
Conversation 1	making copies	borrow a pen
Conversation 2	having lunch	ask the way to the cafeteria
Conversation 3	getting information about courses	get a copy of the class timetable

Section 4
Exercise A
1 forest 2 hill 3 mountain 4 sea
5 lake 6 river 7 island 8 field
Exercise B
1 islands 2 lake 3 mountain
4 sea 5 river 6 forest

Section 5
Exercise A
1 T 2 T 3 F 4 T
Exercise B
1 b 2 a 3 a 4 b 5 a

Section 6
Exercise A
1 c 2 b 3 a 4 b 5 a 6 c
Exercise C
1 are, going to do
2 'm not going to drive
3 're going to save
4 Will, be
5 won't be
6 'm going to join
7 are, going to do
8 're going to make
9 'm going to ride
10 'm not going to use
11 'll do

Listen and write
Exercise B
Person 1: Picture 2
Person 2: Picture 3
Person 3: Picture 1
Exercise C

	1	2	3
Country/City	small island, Greece	Tuscany, Italy	Manhattan, New York City
Natural features / Climate	beach, warm and sunny, clear blue sea	hills, fruit trees, hot summers, warm winters	
Advantages		peace and quiet	won't need a car, good public transportation, cheap places to eat
Disadvantages		lonely	noisy, expensive
Lifestyle activities	morning: go out and catch fish, afternoon: take a nap under a palm tree	live on a farm, grow olives, grow vegetables and flowers	go out to the theater and art exhibitions, eat out every day

DOWN TIME
Exercise A
1 snow 2 island 3 mountain 4 sunny 5 weather
Exercise B
Across
1 island 3 forest 6 mountain 7 clouds / cloudy
Down
2 storms / stormy 4 sunny 5 windy 8 lake

UNIT 10

Section 1
Exercise A
1 have 2 gift 3 decorate 4 guests 5 snacks 6 play
Exercise B
1 invited 2 guests 3 snacks 4 made
5 decorated 6 music 7 gift 8 conversation

Section 2
Exercise A
1 to book a room   4 to buy a new dress
2 to reserve a flight   5 to buy some new shoes
3 to get some money   6 to pack her bag, to rest

Watch out!
She went to Mexico to see her friend.

Exercise B
1 in order to increase   4 in order to let
2 in order to help   5 in order not to disturb
3 in order not to take   6 in order not to make

Section 3
Exercise A
1 crowded 2 relaxed 3 awful 4 lively 5 soft 6 fun
Exercise B
1 Atmosphere: relaxed   2 Atmosphere: lively
Music: soft   Music: loud

Section 4
Exercise A
a
Exercise B
1 c 2 a 3 b

Section 5
Exercise A

Strongly agree	Agree	Disagree	Strongly disagree
I completely agree.	Yes, that's right.	I don't think that's right.	I don't agree.
You're absolutely right.	Yes, that's true.	I'm not sure I agree.	That's not true.

Exercise B
1 agree 2 disagree 3 agree

Exercise C
1 I completely agree.
✗ I don't agree.
2 I'm not sure I agree.
✗ That's not true.
✗ Yes, that's right.
✗ Yes, that's true.
3 You're absolutely right.
✗ I don't think that's right.

Section 6
Exercise A
1 f **2** a **3** c **4** b **5** e **6** d

Exercise B
1 am having, I'll
2 are you going to, We're having
3 We're going, are you going to
4 leaves, It won't take
5 are you doing, I'm going to

Exercise C
1 does, start
2 are, going to wear
3 'll/will wear
4 'll/will have
5 are, going to make
6 'll/will bring
7 isn't coming/isn't going to come
8 's working
9 's going
10 'll/will be

Watch out!
Are you staying at home tonight? / Are you going to stay at home tonight?

DOWN TIME
Exercise A
empty – crowded   quiet – noisy   new – old
large – small   short – tall   stressful – relaxing

Exercise B
boring – dull   lively – exciting   small – tiny
huge – enormous   noisy – loud   terrible – awful

Exercise C
1 loud **2** terrible **3** empty **4** snacks **5** happy
6 small **7** lively **8** large **9** awful **10** guests **11** noisy
Mystery message: Let's have fun!

UNIT 11

Section 1
Exercise A
1 wood **2** glass **3** rubber **4** ceramic
5 metal **6** plastic **7** cotton **8** nylon

Exercise B
1 plastic
2 wood/metal/plastic
3 cotton/nylon/plastic
4 cotton/nylon
5 glass/plastic/metal/rubber
6 wood/plastic/metal/glass/ceramic

Section 2
Exercise A
1 P **2** A **3** A **4** P **5** P **6** A

Watch out!
The table is made of wood.

Exercise B
1 is sold **2** is manufactured **3** are made
4 aren't recycled **5** Are, produced **6** is used

Exercise C
1 Plastic and glass are not recycled in my country.
2 Solar energy is used to generate electricity.
3 Computers are used to control the temperature.
4 Cell phones are sold in electronics stores.
5 This app can be downloaded onto your smartphone.

Section 3
Exercise A
b

Exercise B
1 b **2** c **3** a **4** a **5** a

Section 4
Exercise A
1 was taken **2** was made **3** was invented
4 were developed **5** were sold

Exercise B
1 When was the World Wide Web created?
It was created by Tim Berners-Lee in 1989.
2 When were the first iPhones® produced?
They were produced in 2007.
3 When was the Apple® logo designed?
It was designed by Rob Janoff in 1977.
4 When was the computer mouse invented?
It was invented by Douglas Engelbart in 1963.

Section 5
Exercise A
1 back up **2** click **3** install **4** log on
5 type in **6** right-click **7** print out **8** add

Exercise B
1 log on **2** type in **3** install **4** right-click
5 print out **6** click **7** back up **8** add

Section 6
Exercise A
1 printer **2** laptop **3** smartphone **4** coffee machine

Exercise B
3 I guess so. **1** I think … **1** I'm not sure…
3 Maybe. **4** I suppose so. **2** … probably …

Listen and write
Exercise A
1 T **2** F **3** T **4** F **5** DS **6** T

Exercise B
1 in touch with friends
2 directions
3 times of shows or movies
4 reviews of restaurants
5 pictures
6 music

DOWN TIME
Exercise A
1 B, L; microwave **2** A, J; cell phone **3** C, E; hair dryer
4 D, H; mouse **5** G, K; laptop **6** I, F; game console

Exercise B
glass   metal   rubber
cotton   ceramic   plastic
Mystery gadget: camera

UNIT 12

Section 1
Exercise A
1 f 2 d 3 c 4 e 5 b 6 a

B
1 admire 2 have arguments 3 make up
4 get along with 5 share the same values 6 go through

Section 2
Exercise A
1 b 2 b 3 a 4 b 5 a 6 a

Watch out!
If you <u>help</u> me, I will help you.

Exercise B
1 have, try 2 get, don't 3 don't, ask 4 find, talk
5 give, will get 6 will try, call 7 doesn't, won't
8 won't be, go

Exercise C
1 If I <u>don't</u> have breakfast, I can't concentrate.
2 You will feel tired if you <u>don't</u> get enough sleep.
3 We won't get to school on time if we <u>don't</u> leave now.
4 Our parents get worried if we <u>aren't</u> home on time.

Section 3
Exercise A
1 d 2 c 3 e 4 a 5 f 6 b

Exercise B
1 Job security
2 job satisfaction
3 having good friendships
4 help my community
5 have power
6 hard work

Section 4
Exercise A
agree

Exercise B
1 agree 2 disagree 3 disagree 4 agree

Exercise C
5 Actually, I think you're right.
3 I'm not sure about that.
6 Exactly.
2 Yes, that's true.
1 Well, I think …
4 I think you're forgetting that …

Section 5
Exercise A
1 had 2 Would 3 could 4 wouldn't 5 would
6 wouldn't 7 would 8 were

Section 6
Exercise A
1 It is an opportunity to get real-life experience.
2 They can think carefully about what they want to study at college.
3 They can travel to other countries, or find a job.
4 It can be a lot of fun.
5 It helps young people develop confidence and maturity.

Exercise B
Suggested answer
Many young people take a year off before they start college. It is an opportunity to get real-life experience. For example, they can travel to other countries, or find a job. Also, they can think carefully about what they want to study at college. In addition, it helps young people develop confidence and maturity. Finally, it can be a lot of fun.

Read and write
Exercise A
1 T 2 T 3 F 4 F 5 F 6 T

DOWN TIME
Across
2 share 3 adventure 8 argument 9 power
Down
friendship 3 admire 4 community
6 make 7 security
Exercise B
1 friendship 2 independence 3 money
4 power 5 security 6 family 7 love